T0123608

# My Proverbs Thirty-Two Woman

A Woman
a Husband
Can Trust

WAYNE KNIFFEN

WESTBOW
PRESS®
A DIVISION OF THOMAS NELSON
& ZONDERVAN

Copyright © 2023 Wayne Kniffen.

All rights reserved. No part of this book may be used or reproduced by any means, graphic, electronic, or mechanical, including photocopying, recording, taping or by any information storage retrieval system without the written permission of the author except in the case of brief quotations embodied in critical articles and reviews.

WestBow Press books may be ordered through booksellers or by contacting:

WestBow Press
A Division of Thomas Nelson & Zondervan
1663 Liberty Drive
Bloomington, IN 47403
www.westbowpress.com
844-714-3454

Because of the dynamic nature of the Internet, any web addresses or links contained in this book may have changed since publication and may no longer be valid. The views expressed in this work are solely those of the author and do not necessarily reflect the views of the publisher, and the publisher hereby disclaims any responsibility for them.

Any people depicted in stock imagery provided by Getty Images are models, and such images are being used for illustrative purposes only. Certain stock imagery © Getty Images.

ISBN: 979-8-3850-1277-0 (sc)
ISBN: 979-8-3850-1278-7 (hc)
ISBN: 979-8-3850-1279-4 (e)

Library of Congress Control Number: 2023922542

Print information available on the last page.

WestBow Press rev. date:  11/29/2023

Scripture quotations marked NKJV are taken from the New King James Version. Copyright © 1982 by Thomas Nelson, Inc. Used by permission. All rights reserved.

Scriptures marked as NLT are taken from the Holy Bible, New Living Translation, copyright © 1996, 2004, 2015 by Tyndale House Foundation. Used by permission of Tyndale House Publishers Inc., Carol Stream, Illinois 60188. All rights reserved.

Scripture quotations marked TPT are from The Passion Translation®. Copyright © 2017, 2018, 2020 by Passion & Fire Ministries, Inc. Used by permission. All rights reserved. ThePassionTranslation.com.

Scripture quotations marked MSG are taken from THE MESSAGE, copyright © 1993, 2002, 2018 by Eugene H. Peterson. Used by permission of NavPress. All rights reserved. Represented by Tyndale House Publishers, Inc.

*My Proverbs Thirty-Two Woman* is dedicated to the memory of the most incredible lady I have ever met or known: Betty Ann (B. A.) Kniffen. I will never break my covenant with you (J.21: meaning Judges 2.1, explained later in further detail).

I found my Proverbs Thirty-Two woman:

> *Who can find a virtuous and capable wife? She is more precious than rubies. Her husband can trust her, and she will greatly enrich his life. She brings him good, not harm, all the days of her life.*
>
> —Proverbs 31:10–12 (NLT emphasis added)

# CONTENTS

# INTRODUCTION

Several years ago I told my brother I was going to write a book about my wife and title it *My Proverbs Thirty-Two Woman*. He quickly, but kindly, reminded me that there are only thirty-one proverbs, not thirty-two. I told him there will be thirty-two by the time I finish writing my book.

Actually, this book will never be finished. The impact my beloved B. A. made on my life will last my lifetime. I will be writing about her as long as I live. How can you finish a book when a new chapter is revealed every day by a memory? You can't. It is not possible. But what I can do, which I've chosen to do, is write as much as I can for as long as I can.

June 9, 1960, was a good day for me. I was almost twelve when my future covenant partner was born. In early childhood, that is a ginormous age difference. In the initial stages of our relationship, I would have random thoughts like these: I was in the sixth grade when she entered this world through the birth canal. I was graduating from high school when she was six years old. When she was a senior in high school, I was thirty, a Vietnam veteran, married with three children, and had been pastoring for six years. I remember on one occasion saying to her, "I sure wish I had met you thirty years ago." What she said in response was funny but sobering: "You would be in jail." That had never crossed my mind until then.

It was going to take many years and a lot of hurt and pain before I understood how important this June day in 1960 would be for my life. The words of Jeremiah must have been written just for me. "For I know the plans I have for you,' says the Lord. 'They are plans for good and not for disaster, to give you a future and a hope'" (Jeremiah 29:11 NLT).

There was a time when I wasn't sure if that verse was for me. Oh, I believed it was true because it is the Word of God, but I wasn't convinced it was applicable for me. You see, I jumped the gun and married when I was eight days from turning twenty-one. It was a huge mistake on my part. At that time I was not emotionally or spiritually mature enough to be anyone's husband. The sad thing is, I knew it at the time but followed through with it anyway. Deep inside my innermost being, I knew I was making the wrong choice, but I was not man enough to admit it. For years I thought I would pay for this decision the rest of my life. I was convinced I would never have or ever know what it would be like to be in a covenant relationship with someone I love and have her love me back unconditionally. I was not convinced that kind of relationship really existed. My hope of ever being happy in marriage had been flushed down the drain. And I was the one who flushed it.

The first six words of Proverbs 13 described me to a tee: "Hope deferred makes the heart sick" (Proverbs 13:12 NLT). My hope, my confident expectation of having a great marriage had been delayed. It had been postponed, and not because of anything God had done but by my choice. It was no one's fault but my own. I lived with the consequences of that choice for thirty-one years.

Every time I heard someone brag about his or her marriage, I found it hard to believe. I would think, *Sure you do. We can't see what goes on behind closed doors.* I was suspicious of anyone who claimed to have a great marriage. My basis for feeling and thinking this way came from my experience. I was judging all marriage relationships by mine. Since my marriage was not good, I doubted anyone could honestly say they had a good marriage. I was wrong—so wrong. For twenty-one years I was married to the woman of my dreams. She exceeded my expectations of what a good marriage partner should be and what a healthy marriage really looks like. I am one happy man. The Word of God is true: "A good woman is hard to find, and worth far more than diamonds. Her husband trusts her without reserve, and never has reason to regret it" (Proverbs 31:10–12 The Message). All I have to say to that is amen!

I take great pleasure in introducing you to the love of my life: My Proverbs Thirty-Two Woman, Betty Ann Kniffen (a.k.a. B. A.).

# 1

## *She Made the First Move*

THE HALLWAYS INSIDE OUR CHURCH FACILITIES WERE BUZZING with people traffic. Most everyone who entered the building was engaged in small talk with those they were bumping elbows with. People were happy to see one another. As they passed the administration area, most smiled and waved. Some cracked the door open to say hello to those of us who were still inside taking care of last-minute details for our Wednesday night ministries. Most of the time you would find me in my office gathering what I thought I would need for the service. I always left my office door open so people could come and go as they wished. The thing I enjoyed most about our services was the family atmosphere, the informality that was present in our midweek meetings. I loved when children walked into my office unannounced to tell me hi, grab a treat from the candy bowl, and run. Sometimes I pretended I was going to run them down, wrestle them to the floor, and take my candy back. That's what I told them I was going to do. They laughed and squealed as they ran away.

This particular Wednesday evening was no exception. All of the above was in play when she stopped by my office on her way to the prayer meeting. Because the door was open, she just walked in. I was shuffling through a pile of papers on my desk; all the while, she paced back and forth, talking. To this day I can't remember much of what she said. But I vividly remember her last statement: "I'm in love with you."

Everything I had taken off my desk went crashing to the floor. Papers scattered everywhere. Stunned and shaken, I told her that what she was feeling was just that—feelings. It is not uncommon for a counselee to think he or she has fallen in love with the counselor; patients may think they are in love with their physician. But these emotions pass in time. I told her that what she thought she was feeling for me was not love but infatuation.

She turned to walk out of my office, and she looked over her shoulder and said, "Whatever."

I did everything I could to appear calm and in control of my emotions, but inside I was rattled. I was in a state of shock. *What in the world had just happened?* A lady I only knew by name had just walked into my office and told me she was in love with me. This only happened in movies or soap operas. The last thing I wanted or needed was a love affair.

Two months prior to this I had called a special meeting with my church family so I could tell them I had been served with divorce papers. With almost twenty-five years of pastoring under my belt, I've faced many situations that were tough, but this one topped the list. I was convinced that my long tenure as pastor of this wonderful church was over, maybe even my ministry. What about our community? How would they respond? News can break the sound barrier in a small town, especially if it is juicy. And most of the time it gets tainted and twisted as it is passed from one ear to another.

Divorce is a severe wound for ministers, and it oftentimes determines their future. To my utter amazement, the people I had been with for almost twenty years asked me to stay. My emotions were still fragile, but I agreed to remain as their pastor. But it was not long before I knew in my heart of hearts that the best thing for me and the church was to leave. I was emotionally drained, and the people of the church were constantly defending their decision for asking me to stay as their pastor.

There's not much room in the ministry for those who have been divorced, whether justified or not. Divorce is the scarlet letter of ministry. I now found myself in a situation that I had been critical and judgmental about for most of my ministry—those who had been divorced, especially pastors. How can you trust someone as your pastor when he or she can't take care of his or her own marriage? Why would you want to?

I lived under that guilt for almost thirty-one years. I had great success in helping countless numbers of couples stay together, but I could not save my own marriage. I was a fraud; at least that's what the enemy used to beat me down in his attempt to take me out of the ministry. Little did I know this was actually the launching of my ministry. What the enemy uses to take you out, God can use to set you free. It all depends on how you look at it and how you respond when things seem to be going south.

## The Gathering Place

It was common for people from our church to gather at a local restaurant following the Sunday evening service for a time of fun, food, and fellowship. Anyone and everyone had a standing invitation to be part of this group. It was an enjoyable and laid-back atmosphere. Some of the best times were when someone paid for your meal. And it happened occasionally.

When I walked into the restaurant on that particular evening, the first person I saw sitting there with her three-year-old daughter was Betty Ann. This was the lady who had told me she was in love with me. Since everyone saw me walk into the restaurant, it would be obvious that something was wrong if I turned and ran. That thought did cross my mind. Emotionally, I had slipped on my Jonah sandals. I felt uncomfortable being in her presence, even though there was a crowd sitting at the same table. What kind of conversation would we have? I certainly was not going to mention the short exchange we'd had in my office a few weeks earlier. No sirree! My concern was that she might bring it up. *How will I respond if she does? What will I do? Where will I go?* My thoughts were splattering all over the place. Needless to say, I ate lightly that evening.

Our Sunday evening gathering at the local eating establishment was not the only place I saw Betty Ann on a regular basis. She was also part of our prayer ministry team. After the Wednesday evening meetings were over, five or six of us met in the auditorium for prayer. During our time together, every person on the prayer ministry team prayed out loud. I was always moved by this lady's prayer life. She did not pray like the normal Christian. When she prayed, she dug deep down where most people never go, or even want to go. She grabbed hold of the hem of the Lord's garment. Everyone loved it when it was her time to talk to the Lord, because when she prayed, the entire atmosphere changed.

There was never a time when this lady stepped over the boundaries of our prayer ministry protocol. She never expressed her feelings toward me by a look or by words. Even though she kept her feelings to herself, I always felt a little uncomfortable when the prayer team met. How weird, warped, and ungodly it is to be on the same prayer team with someone you really don't know who said she is in love with you. It's just not right—especially if it's between the pastor and a parishioner. Again, there was nothing untoward going on between us. The only thing I knew about this lady was her name.

## Rumors Started by Dirty Laundry

During one of our Sunday night gatherings at the local hangout, Betty Ann asked me in front of everyone where I did my laundry. This was the first time I had been asked that question. All eyes were locked on me. They seemed to be interested in hearing my answer. I told her I had not done any laundry recently, but I sure needed to.

In front of the entire group, she said, "You're welcome to use my washer and dryer any time you want." She added, "To make you feel at ease, I'll go to the Copelands when you decide to wash and dry your clothes. That way you'll feel more comfortable." Then she told me where I could find the detergent and dryer sheets. I told her thanks, and everyone at the table smiled and nodded.

The time came when I could put it off no longer. I had to get some laundry done. Betty Ann and I agreed on a day and time. Before I went to her house, I fed and watered my horses. On my way back into town, I passed the home of one of our members and noticed several cars parked in the drive. I thought, *I pray nothing bad has happened.* Then it dawned on me that it was one of our lady's life-group meetings. I had a brainstorm. I would have some fun scaring them by scratching on one of the window screens.

After parking my truck, I sneaked up to one of the windows by the front porch. I saw a bunch of ladies sitting around the kitchen table, laughing and having a good time. I decided that it may not be a good idea to carry out my plans to interrupt their time together. Instead, I planned to call when I did laundry and give them a hard time.

When I arrived at Betty Ann's house, the first thing I noticed was that her car was not in the driveway or garage. This was a relief. She was at the Copelands just like she told me she would be. As I was washing my dirty clothes, I made a phone call to the lady who was hosting the women's life group. The house phone was close by, so I used it to make the call. I had no idea, nor did I really care, that the ID of the phone I was using appeared on the phone of the lady I was calling. We engaged in some pleasant chitchat, and then I told her what my plans had been to startle them. But when I peered through the window and saw they were having a good time, I decided against it. After a pleasant conversation, we hung up. I did not give it another thought. I had to finish my laundry.

The rumor mill ratcheted up: *Pastor Wayne is spending time with Betty Ann at her house. He was caught on her phone.* The gossip got its legs from that lady's life group. The leader of that group was present that Sunday night when Betty Ann asked me if I had a place to do my laundry. Before long, rumors were flying around. I got pulled out of one meeting by individuals who demanded that I confess to having an affair. I've had headhunters come after me in my ministry before, but never to this extent. When people are convinced that you are guilty of what is being said about you, there is no way you can defend yourself. When someone does not want to know the truth, nothing you can say will convince him or her otherwise.

During this entire season of insanity, Betty Ann never once lashed out at anyone; she never pointed her finger or accused anyone of anything. She stayed in peace. She lived her life by the principle of time. Time will either indict you or vindicate you … just give it time. And it has. Over the years we've had people call, text us, and send emails, and some have dropped by our home to apologize for spreading gossip that they have found to be untrue. After each contact, I would look at Betty Ann and say, "Time."

All the chatter flying around was actually what drove us closer together. We started having some one-on-one times in public to discuss what was being said and if we could do anything about it. I had already resigned my position as pastor and was in the process of making plans to move to the other side of the state. I did not believe it was possible for me to make a fresh start staying in the area where I was born and raised. If starting a new life was what I needed to do, I would go all the way. My new home would be in the Panhandle of Texas, a place I said I would never live.

At this juncture I did not think our meeting together would add fuel to the fire, but I had reached the point where I really didn't care. We always met in a public venue. During this time, I learned more about this lady than just her name. She was totally opposite from what some had told me. There was something different about her, and I could not put my finger on it. She was different, but in a good way. I never heard her rant or rave about what was going on. Words of anger, negativity, or condemnation never came out of her mouth. She was the antithesis of me. Sometimes we do not need answers, we just need for someone to listen to our incoherent chatter. I am wired differently. You could say I had a *spirit-of-slap* on me. I was ready to fight. Enough was enough.

During my times of anger and frustration, Betty Ann would always say, "People will say what they want to say, believe what they want to believe, and there is nothing that can be done about it."

During my times of venting about how the rumor mill got started, Betty Ann would smile and calmly say, "It's going to be all right. What I told you on that Wednesday night in your office is true. I am in love with you.

I'll have to admit, I was suspicious. I did not want to get back in to what I had just gotten out of, especially this quickly. My life was about to radically change in a way that I would never have imagined. Everything I had ever wanted in a marriage was unfolding before my very eyes, and I was totally ignorant of it.

## Tailgate Testimony

When our relationship seemed to gain momentum, I spilled my guts about my life. You see, I had never allowed anyone to enter the private chambers inside my soul. I was so insecure that I did not want anyone to really know me. It was time for me to do the pacing, like she did in my office on that Wednesday night, only this time she sat on the tailgate of my truck. I walked back and forth and emptied fifty years of my life: the good, the bad, and the not so pretty. I was convinced this would destroy the confidence she had in me. She would not want to risk having a relationship with a flawed man. In a weird way, I was hoping she would see the light and go her separate way.

I had been a pastor for thirty years at the time, and I thought pastors could not share their flaws. Victories yes, but not shortcomings. Who would want to have a pastor who was not perfect?

After hearing my story, I was certain this would be the end of a quick beginning. She would go her way, and I would be left alone to start over.

To my utter amazement she did not blink. All she said was, "Wayne, you're a good man. I told you in your office that I was in love with you. I love you more now than I did then."

For the first time I felt safe in a relationship. No more hiding my feelings, stuffing my shortcomings, or being afraid that people would not love me if they knew I was truly a human being. I cannot tell you how liberating that was. I felt like I had won the lottery. In one way, I had. Betty Ann's unconditional love and belief in me is what made me want to be the man she believed I was.

## Starting Over

It was time. With my pickup loaded with personal belongings, I headed west. There would be a lot of windshield time ahead for me—plenty of time to think, reflect, and face reality. In the rearview mirror I saw the old chapters of my life closing. In the windshield I saw new chapters opening.

Here is what I really believed would happen. I would relocate, and in time, Betty Ann would find someone else and live happily ever after.

Was I ever wrong.

All during my nine-hour drive, she called me just to chat, to see how I was doing, and if everything was OK. Those calls kept me from losing what little sanity I had left. I was leaving everything that I knew and was comfortable with and moving to a place I had said many times I would never live. Welcome home.

Six months after relocating to the Texas Panhandle, my life was about to radically change more than it had already.

All during this time, Betty Ann and I stayed in contact by phone. She had become discontented with where she was and did not know what to do about it. In one of our conversations, I asked her what she thought about moving to the northwest side of Texas where I was living. Long story short, she made another move. I was on the verge of finding out that she really meant what she had said to me in my office on that Wednesday evening. She was in love with me.

Not knowing what her future would hold, she liquidated everything she owned in East Texas and relocated to the town where I was living. Over the next year and a half, we got to know each other better. During this entire time she never once lost her tempter, gave me a what-to-for, pouted, raised her voice to me (or anyone else), or manifested any anger or malice toward anyone. I kept thinking, *It's coming. Just give it time.*

Guess what? It never came. Some nasty things were said to and about her on occasions by a few individuals, but she never ran down the folks who said them or spoke evil of them. I have never seen anyone like her in all my life.

When I speak at marriage conferences, I love to watch the faces of those attending. You can see doubt and unbelief on many in the audience as I brag on my Proverbs Thirty-Two woman. Some cannot believe what I am saying is true. You see, it is hard to believe a person has what you do not have. Our tendency is to judge things based on our experiences. If we do not have it, we are suspicious of anyone who says he does. I've been there, done that.

Human tendency is to judge someone else's story by our story, thinking our story is complete reality. A person's story can change in the blink of an eye, even if he or she feels there is no hope. Always remember, if the only thing you have left is you and the Lord, you have just enough to start over.

## Getting Free

There was a time I did not believe a Christian could be influenced or controlled by demonic spirits. I believed the reason so many believers struggled with their new creation identities was simply because they were immature and had not grown in their faith, if they were always battling the same old issues. I might even put them on my *lost list*. They may say they are Christians, but it was not possible for them to be one if they were unable to overcome their weaknesses. This is exactly what the devil wants us to believe. He wants us to deny his existence and the influence he has in the lives of believers. Many Christians refuse to believe there is a possibility they are being influenced by demonic forces.

Here is an interesting side note. Even though there were things that I battled on a regular basis, I would have never placed myself on the same list that I was quick to place others on. I knew I was a child of God, even though there were things I seemingly could not gain victory over. This is when I began to see why God moved me out of my comfort zone to an area that seemed like another world. God had set me up. It was not the ending, as I had thought, as did some other people. It was actually the beginning of what I had always dreamed of having but did not think would ever come to pass. What the enemy used in his attempt to incarcerate me spiritually, God used to liberate me.

I had not been living in the Texas Panhandle very long when I was asked to speak to the students in a Christian school during their chapel service. This was when I met my best friend, Dorman Duggan. He was the pastor of the church that had the school. We hit it off from the get go. As I look back on how things unfolded, I can see God's hands all over it. During many of our off-the-cuff talks, he would mention *deliverance ministry*. As I just told you, I believed deliverance ministry was not for Christians but for those living in third-world countries, not here in America. Deliverance was for those who did not know better, not for us educated church members. Man, was I in for a learning season.

One day my friend asked me if I wanted to go with him to visit Frank Hammond, who to my surprise, lived less than an hour from us. Dorman and Frank had been good friends for many years. Frank gave all his book rights to Dorman before he was promoted to heaven. Dorman told me he was taking his wife, Jani, and suggested I ask Betty Ann if she wanted to go with us. I did, and she did.

I was so excited to have the opportunity to sit and talk with Frank Hammond face-to-face. I had read his book *Pigs in the Parlor* several times, as have millions all over the world. When we met in his home, we learned his wife, Ida Mae, had recently passed away. We sat around his kitchen table and talked almost the entire day. It was an incredible experience.

After our once-in-a-lifetime visit with Frank, Betty Ann and I decided we needed to go through deliverance individually and then as a couple. We did not want to expose each other to the issues we had struggled with before we met. Neither of us wanted a repeat of what we had gotten ourselves into the first time, especially at our age. It turned out to be one of the wisest decisions we ever made.

Since that meeting with Frank, I have had the joy of leading thousands in deliverance over the last twenty-three years. In 2007, I had the incredible experience to be part of a team that held a mass deliverance service in Uganda, Africa, where thousands were set free from demonic bondage. I have also led untold numbers of people here in the states through deliverance.

What I have discovered is that people are people, and demons are demons, no matter where you go. But we should always keep this in mind: God is God.

Being set free, and staying free, is a personal decision. It all depends on how badly we want to experience the freedom that is part of our spiritual birthrights as children of God. Betty Ann and I were desperate for the reality of that freedom. This is the primary reason we had such an incredible marriage. I thank God she made the first move.

# 2

## The Beginning of Our Covenant Marriage

THAT INEVITABLE MOMENT CAME. I WAS CONVINCED THAT WE were ready to make a lifetime commitment to one another. It was time for me to pop the question.

We had been seeing each other on a daily basis for 547 days, a year and a half. We had taken the risk of exposing the deepest secrets of our lives. We did not want any skeletons hiding in our closets when we made our lifetime commitment. No surprises. We knew the good, the bad, and the not so good about each other. Both of us had gone through deliverance individually and as a couple. Neither of us wanted a repeat of our first marriages, so we were willing to do whatever it took to ensure that did not happen. The desires of our hearts were to have the kind of marriage that we both had dreamed about having for a long, long time. This would be a union of security, trust, openness, vulnerability, communication, commitment, acceptance, as well as spiritual, emotional, and physical intimacy. We were committed to championing one another's strengths and potentials.

I wanted to make this moment special and as memorable as I possibly could. There are no do-overs, so I wanted my proposal to be something we could talk about with fond memories for the rest of our lives together. After a considerable period of time, I made the decision when I was going to ask Betty Ann to marry me, and where I was going to ask her. It would be in the mountains of Colorado during the spring break snow skiing season. I set my sights on the Purgatory Ski Resort in Durango, Colorado. During this time of year it should not be as cold as it is during the winter months, yet the skiing conditions are usually pretty good. I had been there several times and knew the area fairly well. It had become one of my favorite Colorado ski resorts.

## Our Road Trip to Purgatory

With our bags packed, we were Purgatory bound. Betty Ann had no clue where we were going. All during our marriage, I took her places and did not tell her beforehand where we were headed. Until she hooked up with me, her longest road trip had been when she moved from East Texas to the Texas Panhandle. Traveling was not her cup of tea. But she always enjoyed herself when we reached our destination. I never knew her to pay much attention to our location when we were traveling. She seldom read road signs. Most of the time she could not tell you what state we were in.

When the windshield filled with the beautiful Colorado mountains, she was awestruck. If I remember correctly, she said something like, "I didn't know New Mexico had so many beautiful mountains."

I said, "Sweetheart, we're in Colorado."

"We couldn't be. I just saw a sign that says Albuquerque."

"You sure did," I responded. "About three-and-a-half hours ago."

All I got was a smile and, "Oh."

Betty Ann was a hoot to travel with. Even though she seldom knew where she was, she did not care as long as she was with me.

I would ask, "Do you have any idea where we are?"

She would say, "Nope, but you do, and I'm with you."

I laugh every time I think about the time we got separated from our group in Frankfurt, Germany, on our way to Israel. There was not a smidgen of concern on her part. She thought we were in Tel Aviv and that everyone had gone to our hotel or shopping. She didn't know, nor did she care, that we still had a four-hour flight to Israel ahead of us. Her biggest concern was that everyone had gone shopping without us. When it came to shopping, she was the GOAT (greatest of all time).

## She Said Yes

I must admit I was pretty nervous. For an entire week I battled diarrhea caused by a nervous upset stomach. *What will she say when I ask her to marry me? Surely, she will say yes. But what will I do if she says no?*

Even though I had gotten to know her well, my past marriage experience would still get in the way occasionally. I would be bombarded with thoughts like, *Will this marriage be what I hoped it will be, or will it be full of painful surprises? What will happen when we are faced with unforeseen challenges? Would this expose a side of Betty Ann the enemy had tried to convince me was there, but I never saw?* I had no reason to believe there would be, but who knows what the future will reveal?

My experience with pain was trying to rob me of my present peace. Capturing my thoughts became a persistent discipline. I just did not want to repeat the same mistake I made thirty-plus years earlier. I was mature emotionally and spiritually enough now to call it off if I needed to. I am so thankful that I listened to the prompting of the Holy Spirit and not the voices that were occasionally infiltrating my thought life. In all the years Betty Ann and I were married, I never once saw any of those counterfeit thoughts manifest that the enemy had tried to plant in my head.

After spending an incredible day skiing the slopes of the beautiful mountains in Purgatory, I decided I would ask Betty Ann to marry me when we had dinner that night. All day long I had been thinking about how I would frame the words that I would say to her, what the moment would look like, and what her answer would be.

That evening was like something you would read in a romance novel, except for one thing. The words that I had rehearsed on the ski slopes did not come out the way I thought they would, nor as smooth as I had envisioned them to be.

She beamed with a wide smile, squeezed my hand, and without hesitating, said, "Yes, I would love to be Mrs. Wayne Kniffen."

I can't describe the peace that flooded my soul at that moment. I knew in my "knower" that this was the right decision. Asking Betty Ann to marry me was the second-best decision I have ever made. The best decision was when I accepted and received Jesus Christ as my Lord and Savior in 1968 when I was serving in Vietnam.

Because of the poor choices we had both made in our past, it took a lot of years and caused us a lot pain and grief to get us to this point in our lives. This was the beginning of the kind of marriage both of us had longed for but never thought we would have. God was giving us another chance to get it right. We were being given the desires of our hearts. And we both knew it.

I keep a picture of Betty Ann next to my computer so I can look at it every day. It makes my eyes water every time I see it. She was so beautiful and full of peace and joy. The picture was taken in Purgatory, Colorado, the day after I asked her to marry me. Her face has a radiant glow that was a reflection of her soul. She was ready for me to be her lifetime marriage covenant partner, and I wanted her to be mine.

## The Planning of Our Covenant Marriage Ceremony

It was time to make wedding plans. We both knew what we wanted in order to make the ceremony special from start to finish. We had talked about it extensively. It was the center of our prayer focus. Our desire was for it to be a testimony to the faithfulness and goodness of our God. We were living proof that when you own up to your mistakes, and put God first, you set yourself up for His blessings. Our testimony became the prop God used on numerous occasions to hold up a lot of sagging marriages over the years.

Our first purchase was rings. I did not give her a ring when I proposed. A ring is something you wear for a long time, so I wanted us as a couple to pick out the one that she would be proud to wear on her left hand. After a lot of searching, we found it. I did not buy it at that time. I had a plan in mind. I'm always scheming, in a good way. I could tell she was a little disappointed that we did not get it that day. My plan was to surprise her with it—you guessed it—at our favorite burger joint, Whataburger. (You can read more about this incredible event in the last chapter of this book.)

Not only would there be a giving and receiving of wedding rings during the ceremony, we would also exchange covenant rings that would be worn on the ring finger of our right hands. Inside our covenant rings, we had Ecclesiastes 4:9–10 inscribed, which says, "Two are better than one, because they have a good reward for their labor. For if they fall, one will lift up his companion. But woe to him who is alone when he falls, for he has no one to help him up" (New King James Version). These rings were a constant reminder that we were in a lifelong covenant with one another. They were and are still very special to me. I will continue to wear mine as long as I'm alive. It is a constant reminder that even though death has temporarily separated us physically, the covenant we made to each other remains intact.

We also wanted to have a special moment in our wedding ceremony for a salt covenant exchange. I will have to admit this was Betty Ann's idea, even though I want to take credit for it. Each one of us had a small pouch filled with salt. At a specific time in the ceremony, I took salt from my pouch and placed it into her salt pouch. She did the same. This was to signify the sealing of our marriage covenant. In order to break this covenant we were entering into, we must be able to go into our covenant partner's salt bag and retrieve every grain of salt we put into it. Your covenant partner must do the same.

As you can tell, covenant became really important to Betty Ann and me. Not many marriage partners understand covenant. Covenant is a sealed agreement, a sacred commitment between two people for a lifetime. It is a binding agreement where two parties agree to be totally committed to one another for as long as they live. In all our years of marriage, we never had a trust issue. Never. That is worth its weight in gold. It's not hard to be faithful to someone who loves you in season and out, someone who not only made a *commitment* to be with you but *wants* to be with you. This was a game changer.

We also wanted a scripture that emphasized and reminded us of our commitment to one another. We chose Judges 2:1. "I will never break my covenant with you" (NKJV). We signed all our love notes and texts with J.21. It was our way of saying that we would never break the covenant we made to one another. It represents our oneness. On one of our anniversaries, I had a special necklace made for her with J.21 inscribed on it. It became one of her most treasured possessions.

Our entire wedding ceremony had a covenant theme. This meant so much to both of us. Our desire was to have a union of oneness. And we did for our entire marriage.

### Honeymoon Plans Revealed

Even though Betty Ann was thirty-nine at the time we married, she was naive and gullible in so many ways. She had no clue that I had made reservations for an eight-day, seven-night stay in Cancun, Mexico, for our honeymoon. It was hard to keep it a secret, but I managed to. I told her on the way to catch our plane that I was borrowing my friend's trailer so we could spend our honeymoon camping in the Palo Duro Canyon State Park.

She smiled and said, "OK." There was no excitement in her OK. I could tell camping was not at the top of her favorite list. But she was willing to do it, because we would be together.

During our steak dinner that evening, I told her where we were actually going. The girl literally shouted when I handed her a plane ticket and map of Cancun. I'm not sure if it was the trip to Mexico that brought on the shout, or the relief she felt knowing we were not spending our honeymoon camping. Just saying, we have shared this story many times at marriage conferences and retreats. It always triggers elbow punches and quick looks by those in attendance.

Our honeymoon in Cancun was beyond our expectations. This was Betty Ann's first time to travel out of the country. She loved it. We spent our mornings eating breakfast under a cabana overlooking the ocean. Our days consisted of swimming and taking leisurely strolls on the beach. We usually had an incredible lunch at an outside dining area. The meals we enjoyed during the evenings were beyond description.

During our stay, Betty Ann would look at me and say, "You did good, cowboy. You did good." My beloved covenant partner was always quick to show her appreciation.

## Well Begun Is Half Done

Our time in Cancun came to an end, but our honeymoon continued for twenty-one years. Many things start off well but end up a train wreck, especially marriages. Do you remember me sharing with you earlier how the enemy tried his best to plant thoughts of doubt in my head about Betty Ann's true identity? Thoughts like, *Is she really the kind of person that she presents herself to be? Just give it time; her real self will be exposed. When the time is right, you will see what she is truly like inside.*

Let me tell you what I found out. She was even better than I thought. During our entire marriage I never saw a flaw in her character. Not one. People who really knew her referred to her as being legit. She was the real deal. When she told me she was in love with me in my office on that Wednesday evening, she meant it. Time validated her confession. We loved and cherished each other till death parted us. I will always be in love with my Proverbs Thirty-Two woman.

There is no price you can place on having the freedom to share any and everything with your spouse and not have her blow up and run away emotionally or physically. To have your covenant partner roll up her sleeves and join you in solving a problem is priceless—even when the problem you are trying to resolve was created by a poor choice you made. This is when you are doing life together. And this is the way things should be if you are in covenant. Fewer and fewer poor choices will be made when this becomes reality in a marriage. Great strength comes to a marriage when we are willing to fight *with* our soulmates, not against them.

Let me share with you what Betty Ann and I had on our list of priorities as husband and wife. I am convinced that the oneness we enjoyed was the fruit of the seeds we chose to plant. We will get out of our marriage what we sowed into it. Seed will bear after its kind (Genesis 1:11 NKJV).

## We Had a Covenant of Trust

I'm going to say something that goes against the grain of what most people believe about trust. Trust is given before it's earned. If not, then trust is conditional. If your first kneejerk reaction is disbelief, you may have a trust issue with your spouse. Trust is believing in someone and having confidence in that person's character. Without trust, there can never be a bond of oneness between a man and woman. The one thing soulmates have is trust. Without it, marriage will be hard at best.

Betty Ann had absolute trust in me and I in her. Let me give you an example. During the height of the COVID season, we both had to personally deal with it. I was concerned about her because her immune system had been terribly compromised by 109 chemo treatments and twenty radiation treatments. I decided to take some ivermectin (then touted as a Covid-19 cure) for myself and asked if she wanted some too. She had no idea that you draw ivermectin from a vile with a syringe.

Being full of tomfoolery, I thought I would play doctor and mess with her. After drawing some out, I went to where she was sitting and asked her if she wanted the injection in her hip or arm.

She looked at me with a concerned stare and said, "I don't want it in my hip." Leaning toward me with her shoulder lifted, she said, "Just put it into my arm."

That brought tears to my eyes. I lost it emotionally. That's how much my Proverbs Thirty-Two woman loved and believed in me. That kind of trust made me want to live up to her expectations. She had confidence that I would not do anything to intentionally hurt her. She had unequivocal confidence in me and that I always had her best interest at heart. Being vulnerable to your marriage partner is not comfortable, but it is the only way to ensure a healthy marriage union.

My mind seldom shuts down. I have been called a dreamer for most of my life. They were probably right, but I saw myself as being a visionary. One of my passions is horses. I have had a deep affinity for horses for as long as I can remember. There is something about a horse that is hard for me to resist. I knew what I wanted, or thought I did, but was not sure if I would ever achieve my dreams.

Betty Ann knew my passion for equine. When I was given an opportunity to acquire a specific horse, I bounced it off my beloved.

Here is what she would say to me every time I shared an idea with her: "I trust you cowboy. You have my blessings."

She never once reneged on the confidence she had in me. Because she trusted me, I immediately pumped the brakes on whatever I was thinking about doing. She trusted me, and I did not want to make a decision that would dent our covenant of trust.

## We Had a Covenant of Honor

Honoring one another is a choice that offers great benefits privately and publicly. No one ever heard us demean one other in public, even in jest. That was something we chose not to do. A lot of truth can be spoken in jest, causing irreparable harm to a marriage. We did have some laughs privately. We always honored one other when we were in public. Always.

When we hung out with friends and the parameters of pretension came down, it was not uncommon to hear husbands and wives jab each other with curt remarks.

My covenant partner would preempt the banter going back and forth with something like, "Wayne treats me like a queen. He's always supportive of me, and I can trust him. He makes sure I'm well taken care of. He's so smart!"

I told her privately that I was so thankful she had low standards. She would snicker and say, "I meant everything I said about you."

That created within me a desire to do things for her and be the kind of man she believed I was. We must never underestimate the creative power honor has.

Honoring our covenant partners begins in the home behind closed doors. What is expressed publicly exposes what takes place privately. If you are amazed at what some people say about their spouses in public, can you imagine what is being said in private? What I said about trust is also true with honor. Honor is given before it's earned. If not, then honor is conditional. You honor soulmates when they deserve it—and especially when they don't.

People noticed that Betty Ann and I honored each other. It did not matter if we were in front of people or behind private doors; honor was always expressed. Our closest friends, who knew us for years, have said, "There is no doubt that you guys truly love each other." And they were spot on.

## We Had a Covenant of Communication

Communication is more than just speaking. It is imparting and exchanging information. Sometimes the best way to communicate with your spouse is just listen. Since God gifted us with one mouth and two ears, maybe we should do twice as much listening as speaking. We can learn so much about our covenant partners if we would only listen.

In order to have healthy communication, no subject is off limits. We must be able to talk about anything and everything. This is the risk Betty Ann and I were willing to make in the very beginning of our relationship. It started when she was sitting on the tailgate of my pickup at the horse stables in East Texas. And I am so glad we did. The more we talked about the things we were uncomfortable with, the more we respected and loved each other. Betty Ann was the only one in this earthly realm who really knew me. She was willing to listen to me. She never overreacted to what I said. Her response was always uplifting and positive. She made difficult things easy to talk about. I was never afraid to talk to her about anything.

One of the dreams I had for many years was to go to Israel and be baptized in the Jordan River. That dream became a reality in 2008. After we were baptized, we made our way down to the Dead Sea for a swim. That too was a highly special moment. What made the Dead Sea dead was it had an inlet but no outlet. The Jordan River flowed into the Dead Sea, but nothing ever flowed out. This is what communication is all about. To have a healthy marriage union there must be an inlet and outlet. Healthy communication allows that to happen. Without it, a marriage can become a dead sea. When there is trust and honor in marriage, healthy communication will not be an issue. Good communication keeps the river flowing.

## *We Had a Covenant of Intimacy*

I define *intimacy* this way: In-to-me-you-see. In order for this to happen, there has to be trust, honor, and healthy communication. You become vulnerable when you allow someone to see everything that resides in you.

There are two kinds of intimacy in a marriage covenant: Spiritual and physical. It is important to have them in biblical order. Spiritual intimacy is where we must begin. Physical intimacy will never be an issue when you prioritize spiritual oneness. Physical intimacy is the fruit from spiritual oneness.

Betty Ann and I took communion together at home on a regular basis. We prayed together, and we discussed what Holy Spirit had shown us in our personal Bible studies. We also worshipped together. There is one special moment that I will always remember. The Spirit of God was moving in a big, big way. I had been kneeling for a considerable amount of time praying and seeking God. It was an emotional moment. All of a sudden I felt Betty Ann's hand softly touching my shoulder. It wasn't long before I felt her warm tears dripping down on the back of my neck and the side of my face. Her emotions were intertwined with mine. We were one. I have never felt oneness with anyone like I did with her at that moment. Spiritual intimacy must always be a priority.

Of course, you want to be physically intimate with the one you love and the one who loves you. That gift is God-given. When someone says to his or her spouse, "You think physical intimacy will solve any and all problems," that person is telling you volumes about how he or she sees and feels about the relationship with you. And it is not good.

One of the main reasons Betty Ann and I were able to flesh out these things in our marriage is because of a decision we made at the beginning of our relationship. We believed we would benefit immensely by going through deliverance ministry individually, and then together, because we knew the ending is usually a picture of the beginning. We knew that if we started out right, we would end up right. And we did.

# 3

## *She Was My Safe Place*

HAVE YOU NOTICED THAT MOST MEN HAVE NO PROBLEM sharing their victories? We don't have any difficulties talking about our accomplishments. We will boast about our good rounds of golf, all the incredible shots we made, but will not mention how many golf balls we left in high weeds. Men find it easy to talk about the number of fish they caught, especially the big one that got away. The one that escaped was the biggest of all time. But it's crickets when it comes to talking about how many fishing lures got hung and lost on tree limbs. We don't mind telling you how many times we got a hit in baseball, but don't ask us how many times we struck out.

Here is the problem. The vast majority of men are not comfortable talking about their failures or defeats. The main reason is most men don't have a safe place where they can be vulnerable without being chastised or looked down on. I am a blessed man. My Proverbs Thirty-Two woman provided a safe place for me. I could talk about my victories, my defeats, and my good decisions as well as the bad ones. I never lost her support, nor did I ever lose the confidence she had in me. That was not always the case. Because of the spirit of rejection, I kept my struggles to myself. I refused to allow anyone to know the real me. This is true of most men, and, I might add, women too. Very few people have a safe environment where they have the freedom to share everything—most importantly, their shortcomings. My beloved covenant partner made sure I had that space, and she protected it at all costs. I cannot tell you how freeing that was for me. I made sure to reciprocate that freedom for her.

To be able to share anything with your spouse and not have him or her blow sky high is not common, sad to say. I have referred to what I call my "tailgate moment" with Betty Ann a couple of times already, but I feel a need to share it one more time. Maybe this is more for me than anyone else. I thought for sure she would fly the coop after getting an earful of the real me no one knew. On the outside, people thought I was a brave and confident soul, while on the inside, the real me had feelings of inferiority. I battled with low self-esteem, along with rejection. She listened intently to my divulging what I believed was the real me. I really felt that she would turn tail and run. To my amazement, she didn't. She was able to see in me what I could not see.

This was the beginning of a huge turnaround for me. For the first time in my life I had a safe place where I could be me without feeling I was being judged. That took away my fear of failure and not measuring up to a false standard of success that I had placed on myself. A person is emotionally liberated when he or she feels safe.

## Betty Ann Was a Pure Soul

Like I've already said, I really felt the day was coming when I would see the bad side of Betty Ann. I was convinced that when the conditions were just right, she would explode. There's no way a person could be that good all the time. Well, I was wrong. We were married for twenty-one years, and that side never manifested. It never raised its ugly head because it was not there. It did not exist.

I remember the time when we had a personal one-on-one session with a prophet who said something that was stunning. In the core of my being, I knew he was right. This man had never met us or knew who we were. He said the Lord had given him the gift to see into a person's soul, and that Betty Ann had the purest soul he had ever seen. I lived with this lady and knew what he said was spot on. I know this may be hard to wrap your mind around, but it is the unvarnished truth.

She made home a place I wanted to run to, not from. It was our safe place. We loved being with each other. This lady deserves all the credit for what I have been able to accomplish and become. She gave me the freedom and permission to pursue the desires of my heart. Betty Ann was a paragon of what a loving soulmate should be. As far as I am concerned, I will be in covenant with my Proverbs Thirty-Two woman for as long as I live in this earthly realm.

After Betty Ann was physically unable to oversee her business, we sold her boutique and the beautiful building we had renovated. It was difficult for both of us because this had always been her dream. A lot of sweat-equity had been invested in that business. She owned the prettiest building downtown in our small community of fifteen thousand people.

Four months after we sold the business, Betty Ann went to be with the Lord.

Shortly after Betty Ann's promotion to glory, the new owners contacted me to see if I would join them at the building site for a special time to pay tribute to Betty Ann. They wanted me to know they were following through with the dreams Betty Ann and I had for the business and the building.

It was a moving experience. Several of our city officials were there along with a group of people I did not know, or barely knew. Many tears were shed as people shared personal testimonies about how Betty Ann had helped them and what a blessing she was to so many. One lady, with tears streaming down her face, shared a beautiful story that pegged Betty Ann to the nth degree. She said it was not uncommon to see her sitting on a green bench outside the front door of her shoppe reading her Bible. With her voice cracking while wiping away tears, she said Betty Ann was not ashamed of her Lord. Truer words could not have been spoken about this godly lady. Everyone who knew Betty Ann personally would tell you she was the real deal. She was a pure soul.

## *Betty Ann Always Put Me First*

I never had to wonder where I was on her list of priorities. Everything she did was to support me in whatever I felt the Lord wanted me to do. This made it easy for me to make her my number-one priority too. I wanted to do things for her. Knowing how much she loved me created a desire to treat her like a queen.

After one of her cancer treatments, we had lunch at the restaurant where we had our steak dinner the night of our wedding while waiting to catch our flight to Cancun. At this juncture in her cancer treatments, she was physically weak. She needed assistance to get in and out of our vehicle. No matter where we went, I made sure I pulled the car as close to the front entrance as possible.

This was no exception. After I helped her out of the car and escorted her to the front door, I went to find a parking space. On my way back to help her get inside, a man came running up to me. He asked if I was the one driving the white car. I thought maybe I had parked in the wrong spot, and he was going to ask me to move. When I said yes, he told me my wife had face-planted on the sidewalk.

I ran as fast as I could and was not ready for what I saw. Her left wrist was severally broken and totally bent out of shape. It was close to being a compound fracture. Her face looked like she had been beaten with a baseball bat. This couple graciously helped me get her into our car, and away we went to the emergency room at the closest hospital.

As we waited for the ER doctor, she looked at me and said, "I'm sorry I ruined your lunch."

*What?* Her first thought was about me not having lunch. I could not hold back the tears. Can you believe that? Her main concern was not about herself. She felt it was her fault that we did not get to have lunch. I have shared this story in greater detail at many conferences. It always becomes a special moment in the service. I never had to worry about where I appeared on her priority list.

## *Betty Ann Was My Biggest Fan*

You have something really special when you have someone who is always rooting you on. Betty Ann was my biggest supporter, my biggest fan. She made me believe in myself, that I could do whatever I set my mind to. Not once did she scold me or talk down to me when I tried something new and things did not turn out as well as I thought they would. She had complete trust in me, which made me want to be trustworthy.

If there is anything a man needs from his soulmate, it is emotional support. When a man knows his wife stands behind him no matter what, he becomes more stable and secure. He becomes more cautious in the decisions he makes. He is wiser and more sensitive to the needs of his wife, too. He wants her to feel loved, secure, and protected. When your wife has confidence in you, you never want to violate that trust.

When the Spirit of the Lord began to give me a revelation about our true identities as children of God, people encouraged me to put it into book form. I was hesitant at first. I was not sure that writing was something I wanted to undertake. Writing was never my forte. My sweet wife kept telling me I should listen to what people were asking me to do. She reminded me that God put it in me, and He would help get it out of me. So I began to write, with her encouraging me every step of the way. With her unwavering support, I was able to finish *The Scam*, a book about our spiritual identities as children of God. *The Exchange*, God's quid pro quo, was the second book I wrote. It focuses on how we got our new creation identities. With her constant support, I have written ten more books that have been published. I will keep writing as long as I am in my earth suit. It is amazing what can be accomplished when we are given a safe place.

## *Betty Ann Always Flew under the Radar*

My Proverbs Thirty-Two woman never liked to be in the spotlight. Bright lights always made her uncomfortable. She was happy to remain behind the curtains. She was quick to give others credit for their alms giving, but she did not want anyone to recognize her for what she did for others.

For more than sixteen years my beloved wife owned and operated a highly successful lady's boutique. If you wanted to know what the latest fashions were, all you had to do was talk to Betty Ann Kniffen. She was "knowed-up" on what was in style.

Ladies loved that about her. They had complete confidence in her knowledge of the latest fashions.

After my soulmate went to be with the Lord, I heard story after story about how she helped ladies in our community with clothing. She never discussed those ministry moments with me or anyone else. It was not because she was hiding things from me; her giving to others was done in secret. Her left hand never knew what her right hand was doing (Matthew 6:3–4). She always flew under the radar.

Countless numbers of times she blessed ladies in our town who could not afford an outfit to wear to a funeral, a wedding, or for some special occasion. This was the kind of person I was in covenant with. She had a giant heart full of compassion. I am convinced this is what contributed to her success as a business owner. She legitimately cared for others.

Not only did Betty Ann help women in our town, she was generous to me. I never wanted for a thing. As a matter of fact, I had to be careful about what I said I needed or wanted. Sometimes we may say we want a particular thing, but we really don't, especially men. We are just paying lip service. I call it thinking out loud. She did not take what I said as idle speech. If I said I wanted something, she made sure I got it, no matter how expensive. This taught me to be careful about what I said, because my beloved would make sure I got my heart's desires. She was a giver in every sense of the word. She never forgot how generous her heavenly Father had been to her, so helping others in need came easily.

## Betty Ann Always Affirmed Me in Public

Most people are sensitive when negative things are said about them in public, even if in jest. This is one thing Betty Ann never did. I can't remember one time when she joined in with women who were having fun at the expense of their husbands by gossiping about things they did or did not do at home: "My husband never cleans up after himself." "Sometimes I feel like his slave."

Betty Ann would say, "Wayne treats me like royalty. He always picks up after himself. I'm a blessed woman." She countered negative remarks women made about their husbands with a positive and affirmative statement about me. This created in me the desire to be that kind of husband. It also puffed me up a tad. Just saying.

I never had to worry about Betty Ann running me down or saying derogatory things about me in public, because she never said them about me in private. I never had to worry about her airing our dirty laundry. She always made me feel safe. This did unbelievable things for my confidence and my commitment to be the best husband I possibly could for her. This is another reason I consider Betty Ann to be my Proverbs Thirty-Two woman. My heart trusted her.

## Betty Ann Never Raised Her Voice to Me

When I tell people my wife never raised her voice to me, they look at me in disbelief. The reason they find it hard to wrap their minds around that truth is because it is not their experience. Our tendency is to judge people's experiences and testimonies by ours. If it is not true for us, then it certainly can't be true for anyone else. In other words, been there, done that.

I want to repeat something. Early in our marriage, I was convinced that when the right situation presented itself, she would unwind and explode. Just give it time. Was I ever wrong? In all the years we dated and were married, she never once lost it. She never raised her voice one time.

I have never known anyone like this lady. Betty Ann was one of a kind. I have no reservation in saying she was a gift from God. He knew what I needed so I could fulfill my destiny here on earth. There is no doubt in my mind whatsoever that I am where I am today because of her love, support, and unwavering commitment. I can go to my grave knowing with absolute confidence that great marriages do exist. I was blessed with one. This is why I will continue to wear my wedding band and covenant ring for as long as I live. Betty Ann loved me all the days of her life. I will love her all the days of mine.

Her inner calmness is what the Lord used to settle my over-reactive spirit. Before she and I were in covenant as husband and wife, I felt I had to defend whatever I did. It was a great day when the Lord delivered me from that spirit. I cannot tell you how freeing that was. I had spent the majority of my life in a defensive mode until I met Betty Ann. A defensive spirit comes from feelings of inferiority. She loved me as I was, and this enabled me to become the man God had created me to be. I live in so much peace today because my sweet marriage covenant partner gave me a place where I felt safe.

## Betty Ann Was Not a Complainer

I'm not sure if Betty Ann could spell the word complain. Complaining was not in her nature, and no matter how challenging the situation we faced at the time, she kept a positive attitude. She would say things like, "Together, we can tackle this thing," or "So, let's roll up our sleeves and get it done." And we did! I told her all the time that when I grew up, I wanted to be just like her. All she did was smile and shake her head.

During the first few years, we faced some issues that can be dangerous to the health of a marriage. If it doesn't obliterate the marriage, it can cripple it so it never functions normally. We discussed all this in our "tailgate" conference that we had before we married. We found out rather quickly that you can be forgiven for making poor choices, but you may have to deal with the consequences of those choices, some for an extended period of time. It took us a few years to get some of those issues settled, but we did it together. Tackling these challenges as one only drew us closer in our marriage union. There is no Goliath that can stand against a couple who have chosen to do life together. You don't mind fighting when you have someone who will fight alongside you no matter the odds. We never had to fight a battle alone.

This is why we had Ecclesiastes 4:9–10 inscribed on the inside of our covenant rings: "Two are better than one, because they have a good reward for their labor. For if they fall, one will lift up his companion. But woe to him who is alone when he falls, for he has no one to help him up" (NKJV). For us, this was far more than a scripture that we had hidden in our hearts. It became the mantra of our marriage. God's Word was the cement that held us together as one.

### Betty Ann Was An Encourager

I have never had anyone in my life encourage me more than my precious wife. She was my biggest fan. She really believed I could do whatever I set my mind to. We all need encouragement, but some of us need it more than others. Encouragement is what keeps us on our feet. Betty Ann's constant, unrelenting, "You can do it," kept me standing when I was under the sway of doubt.

About a year before we married, I was thrown a curve ball by someone I thought was my friend. It was devastating. He had been told something about me that was not true from someone he did not know. I thought this was strange because he knew me. The enemy used this lie to sever our relationship. It really rocked me on my heels.

I was approached by a group of guys who asked if I would meet with them at a particular restaurant in a neighboring town to lead them in Bible study. I immediately accepted the invitation. (Teaching the Word of God has been my passion for more than fifty years now.) Our agreement was to meet for six weeks and then evaluate things to see if we wanted to continue. We had a great first meeting. Unbeknownst to me, my used-to-be friend told this group what he had been told by someone, a person he did not even know. When I showed up at our next Bible study, I was the only one there. At first I thought everyone was running late. That is not uncommon for ranchers and farmers; they do not control their schedules. But the longer I waited, the more I realized no one was coming. I still had no clue why.

When I got home, I shared what happened with Betty Ann. I have to admit, I was a little miffed. Well, I was a little more than miffed. I talked things out with my beloved.

She said, "Didn't you commit to meeting with these guys for six weeks? You have four more weeks to go. I suggest you keep the commitment you made, even if no one ever shows."

Guess what I did? Yeppers, I spent four Thursdays at a restaurant in a town thirty miles away, alone in Bible study.

It did not take long before I found out why these men refused to follow through with their commitment to attend our Bible study. They had believed what my used-to-be-friend had said about me. In a short period, almost every one of those guys came to me and apologized for standing me up and for believing the lie. They were amazed that I kept the commitment I had made with them. This did not happen because I was an amazing man of God. My thoughts were on shaking the dust off my sandals and moving on. It was because of the encouragement I received from my precious wife. She always gave me godly counsel. Betty Ann was an encourager.

## From a Tailgate to a Safe Place

All that you have read so far began on the tailgate of my truck. I did not have a clue at the time that God was providing me a safe place—a place I could go to vent, reveal my mistakes, and not be rejected or condemned. It was the beginning of what I always wanted and needed, somewhere I could go to have the freedom to divulge the contents of the secret places in my soul. Betty Ann provided that place for me.

This created a desire to make sure that I provided her a place where she could share the contents of her innermost being without being judged. We became one another's safe place.

# 4

## *She Was a Woman of Faith*

FORGETTING ALL, I TRUST HIM. WHAT A GREAT ACROSTIC FOR the word *faith*. This is faith in its purest form: Forgetting all, I trust Him. The value of people's faith is determined by what they place their faith in. It is possible to have faith in faith. I am convinced this is true for most believers. If this is the case, then we have misplaced faith. This kind of faith has little to no value.

When people say they wish they had more faith, they are telling you how they define faith. They have placed their confidence in faith. Most people are convinced that they could live a victorious life if they had more faith. When this happens, it is easy to get caught up in the comparison hoax: If I had the faith of that person … What we need to ask ourselves is what we are doing with the faith God has given us, and more importantly, what or who we have placed our faith in.

I have never seen anyone exercise and express faith more than Betty Ann Kniffen. She loved the Lord, and her love for Him was evident by the way she lived her life. She would pray for you at the drop of a hat. And when she prayed, you knew you had been prayed for. She found it comfortable with having a conversation with the Lord. It is not hard to talk to someone you love. It is also much easier when you know someone loves you. She loved the Lord, and she knew He loved her.

## *Faith in Action*

One day we were talking about how God had blessed us and how thankful we were that He had given us the desires of our hearts, in having a marriage covenant partner. During our conversation, I asked her what the dream of her heart was. I wanted to know what her lifelong dream had been. Her response was immediate. She had always dreamed of owning her own lady's boutique.

The Lord opened the door for that to become a reality. The initial stages of this new adventure did not happen the way we thought it would, nor the way we would have chosen. After a few years of owning her own business, we were able to see things much clearer. The awkward beginning was a test of character. We were given the opportunity to ask ourselves if this was really her dream. She passed the test with flying colors. God always has His way of doing things. Sometimes His ways may seem weird, but our Father always knows best.

The building where she had her boutique had minor issues with the roof. When it rained, those issues were no longer minor. They became a huge challenge. After many fruitless consultations with the building owner about repairing the roof, we made a decision to buy our own building. Our biggest question was how we would get the financial backing needed to see this dream become a reality.

Every time we talked about what we could and could not do to see this dream come true, Betty Ann would say, "God will make a way." I would smile and give her an affirming nod.

Inside, I was thinking, *It will have to be God, because humanly speaking there is no way.*

She made her stand on Matthew 19:26: "But Jesus looked at them and said to them, 'With men this is impossible, but *with God all things are possible*'" (NKJV, emphasis added). Betty Ann never wavered from believing God would make her dream come true—in His time.

## God Made a Way

One day, a lady who owned a building a few doors down walked into Betty Ann's shoppe. After a brief greeting, this lady asked if we would be interested in buying her building. She and her husband were closing their business because they were retiring. Betty Ann told her she would talk to me about it and get back to her. We placed this opportunity in the crosshairs of our prayers. We wanted to say yes, but we wanted to make sure this was a God deal. We were not going to pull the trigger on this without absolute, settled confidence that we were being led by the Spirit.

Was God making a way for us to own our own building? We certainly wanted to know. Again, the question we wrestled with was how we would finance it. We had no collateral. We had not lived in this town long enough for people to really know and trust us. From a human perspective, it certainly looked like the deck was stacked against us.

With unwavering faith, Betty Ann continued saying, "God will make a way."

After contacting the lady about the possibility of us purchasing their building, a meeting was set up with her and her husband to discuss it. During this meeting we were told what they were asking for the building. I countered their asking price several times, but they would not budge.

I really did not know what to do until I saw the look on my sweet beloved's face. "We'll take it." Those words came out of my mouth quickly and unabated. What I said brought a sweet peaceful smile to Betty Ann's face and a *what in the world did I just say?* to mine.

As we walked down the street back to my wife's shoppe, I said: "Well, we made a commitment to buy their building with money we don't have."

You guessed it: "God will make a way," was her response.

What in the world were we going to do? If this dream was going to become a reality, it would certainly have to come from the hand of God. Without divine intervention, we made a commitment we could not live up to.

We needed to do something that should have been done at the beginning of this dream: visit a lending institution to find out how much money we could borrow before we made a commitment to purchase anything. For some reason we visited an independently owned local bank. Don't ask me why. This was not where we did our personal banking. We did not know a soul who worked at this bank.

After being escorted into the office of one of the lending officers, we shared our vision and our need. I just knew we were going to be asked what we had for collateral that would put this loan on a solid foundation. That question was never asked. I was mystified. Within thirty minutes we had signed the loan papers and had a check in hand for enough to buy the building at the seller's asking price, and to totally renovate it.

As we drove away from the bank, Betty Ann placed the check on her knee so I could take a picture of it. We were both taken aback by what had just happened. It was obvious to us that this was God's doing. He had made a way when there seemed to be no way. Betty Ann had been telling me He would.

We had made an agreement with the bank that we would pay the loan back in fifteen years. God blessed the business so much that we were able to pay off the bank note in half that time. From start to finish we had no doubt whatsoever that this business was from the hand of God. It was my dear wife's pulpit. She had the freedom to minister to the ladies who came into her shoppe without any reprisals. God honored her faith and gave her the dream of her life. The strange beginning of her business was for us to see if we could be trusted. There was never a doubt if we should or should not have pursued Betty Ann's vision of owning her own boutique. God had made a way.

## Betty Ann Kept Containers Fille With What She Was Believing God For

We had not been living in the Texas Panhandle for very long when we began to talk about the possibility of buying some land to build our future home on. The property that had captured our attention was a parcel of land just outside the city limits. But there was only one thing wrong; it was not for sale. I never believed it would be because the owner planted wheat on it to graze cattle.

One day as I was passing this parcel of land, I could not believe what I was seeing. There was a for sale sign on this prime piece of property. The owner was selling this half section of land in five-acre plots. The possibility of us owning five acres of this land made me salivate.

I immediately called Betty Ann to give her the news. She could not believe it either. I told her that I did not know what the land was selling for, nor did I have any idea how we could afford to buy any of it.

Guess what she said? Yep: "If it's a God deal, He will make a way."

Many people in our area had the same feelings about this land as we did. It began to sell, and sold quickly. There were only two five-acre tracts left. Beautiful homes were already being constructed. It looked like we were going to miss out.

For a couple of years we stopped to look at the land and walk around on part of it. As we walked, we prayed. Little did I know what Betty Ann was doing. She was scooping up some of the dirt and placing it in a small container. Every day she prayed over the dirt that was kept in a ceramic vase. Her faith was not focused on the dirt in the container but on the One who created the dirt.

I knew I had to act quickly or we would miss out on this opportunity that had been miraculously presented to us. I made a call to enquire about the land. After that phone call, we did not own five acres of this prime property—we owned ten. We were excited and stunned at the same time. Again, God had made a way. The loan for this property was for ten years. But God provided a way for us to pay it off in five. My covenant partner was a woman of faith. She believed God would provide for us. And He always did.

I could tell you story after story about Betty Ann's walk of faith. She was an amazing lady. But I think I would be less than honest if I did not mention some of her defects. Yes sir, she had some chinks in her armor.

## Betty Ann Had Some Defects

Up to this point it may sound like I am presenting Betty Ann as someone who was perfect, who had no flaws or blemishes. She was a tremendous person, but believe it or not, she had some issues. The lady would eat just about anything. When I say anything, I mean anything. I don't think there was any type food she would not try. I first noticed her eating disorder when we were celebrating one of our anniversaries at a nice restaurant. When she told the waiter that she wanted liver and onions, I almost fell out of my chair.

"Did I just hear you order liver and onions?" She smiled and nodded. She could have had a steak, but she ordered—you know. To make a bad moment even worse, I had to pay for her meal! It was expensive, too. But I did love my liver-eating covenant partner.

Not long after we were married, we attended a cutting horse event in Ft. Worth, Texas. On our way to the cutting, our conversation was focused on eating. We talked about how nice it was going to be to have all the different types of foods that would be available for us to choose from. Every place we named sounded really good. We finally chose a really nice restaurant that we had heard about for years. It was known for its delicious ribeye steaks and chicken-fried steaks.

When the waiter came to take our order, guess what my beloved requested? She did not order a ribeye or a chicken-fried steak; she ordered mountain oysters. I was raised in the country and love country cuisine, but mountain oysters? Nope! It ain't happening. She did not get a kiss from me the rest of the evening. I do have my limits. The woman would try anything.

As we made our way through Austin, Texas, several years ago, Betty Ann and I made the decision to eat at a seafood restaurant known for its amazing food. They serve some of the best seafood I have ever eaten. Just about everything on their menu is off the charts. I ordered the captain's platter, which is their specialty. It was phenomenal. If you are still hungry when you leave, it is your fault.

When the waitress asked my wife what she would like to order, she said, "I'd like the raw oysters, please." Raw oysters! Not in this lifetime.

I cannot count the times she would have me stop at a place in Amarillo, Texas, to get her some fried chicken gizzards. This was one of her favorite snack foods. I would roll down my window so the smell that had permeated the cab of my truck could escape.

Every time she took a bite from her chicken gizzard snack-pack, she looked at me, smiled, and said, "You want one?"

I'll bet you can guess what my answer was.

My beloved Betty Ann had to be a woman of great faith to eat what she did. When it came to eating strange foods, she had no qualms about giving it a try. This is the prayer she prayed over her meal, "Bless the Lord, O my soul, *and all that is within me,* bless His holy name" (Psalm 103:1 NKJV, emphasis added)!

When it comes to liver, mountain oysters, raw oysters, and chicken gizzards, my prayer is, "Lord, increase my faith." Since He hasn't, I'll leave that cuisine to those who have great faith.

## Betty Ann's Faith Was Expressed through Her Prayer Life

My favorite person to hear pray was Betty Ann. When she prayed, her faith drilled deep into God's reservoir of provisions. The sincerity of her spirit could be felt when she conversed with the Lord. It is amazing how many people over the years have called her asking for prayer about specific things. People knew she had a serious and legitimate prayer life. If you asked her to pray for you, she thought you meant it. I was blessed to have her as my prayer partner. She was a prayer warrior. When Betty Ann prayed, she declared war, and she fought to win. She did not believe in taking hostages.

For a period of time, the Lord opened the door for me to travel, primarily overseas, to share the message about our spiritual identities as new creations in Christ. It was so comforting to know that she had my back in prayer. I never had any doubt that she kept me and my team in her heart and on her lips when she talked to God. There were moments in Africa when things looked like they had the possibility of getting out of hand. When the enemy raised his old ugly head, we felt the presence of God's peace. It was as if we were walking in a prayer bubble. My sweetheart prayed a hedge of protection around me and the team. What we have been able to accomplish in ministry must be attributed to my prayer partner. She was a great woman of faith, and she expressed her faith through prayer.

## Betty Ann's Faith was Expressed by the Way She Treated Her Enemies

We all know from experience how easy it is to love those who are easy to love, and those who love us. But loving those who are difficult to love is another story. As long as I knew Betty Ann, she never held a grudge against anyone. Matthew 5:43–44 was not just a passage of scripture she knew in her head, it was something she fleshed out in her life.

> You have heard that it was said, "You shall love your neighbor and hate your enemy. But I say to you, love your enemies, bless those who curse you, do good to those who hate you, and pray for those who spitefully use you and persecute you." (NKJV)

It was a sobering day when my mother passed away. It was a reminder how brief life really is. We are here today and gone tomorrow. With all her faults, my mother loved her kids to a fault.

She also thought the world of my precious wife. At our wedding, my mother told me she hoped I knew how blessed I was to be marrying Betty Ann. That was another confirmation that we were making the right decision to become husband and wife.

At my mother's memorial service, a family member said something nasty about Betty Ann when she walked by. It was vicious and demonic.

When Betty Ann told me about it, I asked her how she responded. She said, "I kept walking and praying."

All the years we were married, Betty Ann never stopped praying for this person. She never allowed anyone to live rent free in her head. It was evident she was a woman of faith by the way she treated her enemies. She blessed those who cursed her.

## Betty Ann's Faith Was Expressed through Her Quiet Spirit

She had the sweetest spirit of anyone I have ever met. A quiet spirit is not to be construed as weakness; it is actually a strength. A quiet spirit is not easily distracted or provoked. The reason Betty Ann never ran anyone down publicly is because she never did it privately. Her quiet spirit manifested her character, not reputation.

One day we were in a four-way conversation with some friends. The conversation had degenerated to a low level. A certain individual we all knew was being fried by loose talk and unsubstantiated accusations. Everything being said was based on hearsay. Betty Ann maintained her quiet spirit during the entire conversation. When we were alone, I asked her why she did not say anything.

Here is what she told me: "You can never take back what you say, good or bad." She was so right. You can't *un-spill* spilled milk.

She always thought about something deeply before she said anything. We were as opposite as you can possibly be in this area. I had a history of overloading myself with quick, rash statements or comebacks. My mouth has gotten me in trouble more times than I want to remember. Betty Ann's quiet spirit impacted my life for the better. Today, I am able to harness my mouth so much better than I once did. What I say and when I say it is more controlled, all because of the impact my beautiful covenant partner had on me. She was a lady of faith, and her faith was expressed through a quiet spirit.

## Betty Ann's Faith Was Expressed through Her Giving

I had always felt I was a generous giver, until I met my Proverbs Thirty-Two woman. When it came to giving, this lady was over-the-top with her generosity. She was incredibly benevolent. She taught me that there is giving, and then there is giving! I saw her giving spirit in action.

Over the years I have tried to expose the people I have pastored to the five-fold ministry gifts, apostles, prophets, evangelists, pastors, and teachers in order for us to be as spiritually healthy as possible. On one occasion we had a prophet friend from South Africa come for a Sunday through Wednesday meeting. During each service, we gave our people the opportunity to give a love offering so we could bless this person. Our people were always generous with their giving.

Betty Ann and I would pray about what our gift should be for our guest speaker. On the last day of the meeting, we shared with each other what we believed it should be and then gave it. I usually had in mind what I considered a very generous gift. But she always, and I mean always, had a larger gift on her heart.

We went with what she believed we should give. You can never out-give God.

Later that afternoon I got a phone call from Betty Ann. I thought something bad had happened because she was crying. When I ask her what was wrong, she said, "The Lord just told me that we should double our gift."

I was speechless. Trying not to lose control of my emotions and appear like an unbeliever, I cleared by throat and said, "Sure." When we hung up, I sat in my desk chair in a state of shock.

What in the world had just happened? We had given some large gifts in the past, but none of them came close to matching this one. To make this short story even shorter, we were obedient and gave.

It wasn't long before God poured His favor into our laps. We ended up getting far more than we have given. It was pressed down, shaken together, and running over.

Betty Ann was a woman of faith, and her faith was expressed through her giving. She always believed God would provide. And He always has.

# 5

## *She Was a Woman I Could Trust*

IF THERE IS ANY ONE THING A MARRIAGE NEEDS FOR IT TO BE healthy and successful, it is trust. Unequivocal trust is the soil in which a healthy and sustainable marriage grows and matures. Without trust, you have all the ingredients for a ticking time bomb. If trust ever becomes an issue in a marriage, it's not a matter of if it implodes but when.

Betty Ann and I had trust issues from our pasts when our relationship began to bloom. The deliverance ministry that we submitted to took care of that. This is another reason I am convinced that couples, married or those thinking about marriage, need to go through freedom ministry. Without realizing it, people will usually drag all their hurts and pains of the past into their present, which will affect their future in a big way. Trust issues don't go away just because you remarry. They can actually be enhanced.

The devil wants you to believe there is no one you can really trust. I'm here to tell you he is a liar, just like Jesus said he is (John 8:44). Satan's greatest weapon is a person's ignorance.

Until trust issues are resolved, we will live our entire lives behind emotional walls that we have erected in our attempt to protect ourselves. We see it as self-preservation. We are not going to allow anyone behind these walls, because if we do, we will be vulnerable to more hurt.

If our previous marriages had trust issues, we may feel that protecting and guarding our feelings must be a priority. What really happens is we isolate ourselves and miss out on opportunities for true happiness. The ability to protect oneself from being hurt emotionally, or rejected, is not a strength; it is a weakness. If you don't know who you are as a new creation in Christ, you must defend yourself. When you know your identity in Christ and your birthright privileges, you will not feel the need to defend yourself. You allow the Holy Spirit to defend you.

As Baptist preacher Charles Spurgeon said, "The Word of God is like a lion. All you have to do is let the lion loose, and the lion will defend itself." This is something Betty Ann believed and lived. We looked to Jesus as our example.

There is another element that is so easy to overlook when it comes to issues of trust in a marriage. If we don't have confidence in ourselves, how can we have confidence in someone else? Not being able to trust ourselves is a sneaky snake. It hides cleverly disguised in the shadows of our thought lives.

Not trusting oneself has never crossed the minds of most people. It falls into the same category as loving others. Listen to what Jesus said about love.

> Jesus answered him, "The first of all the commandments is: Hear, O Israel, the Lord our God, the Lord is one. And you shall love the Lord your God with all your heart, with

all your soul, with all your mind, and with all your strength. This is the first commandment. And the second, like it, is this: *You shall love your neighbor as yourself.* There is no other commandment greater than these." (Mark 12:29–31 NKJV, emphasis added)

When Jesus answered the scribe's question about what the greatest commandment was, He covered all the bases. We are to love God with everything we have. Then *we are to love our neighbors the same way we love ourselves.* Pay close attention to what Jesus said. It is impossible for us to love others if we don't have proper self-love. But it must begin by loving God with our entire beings. When this happens, we will love others the way we should, because we have a healthy love for ourselves.

Instead of the word *love,* let's use the word *trust.* It reads like this: Trust others as you trust yourself. If we have a problem trusting others, we may have an issue trusting ourselves. That is something that never crosses the minds of most people. Loving others is proportionate to the way we love ourselves. Trusting others is proportionate to the way we trust ourselves.

Let me repeat what I said in chapter 2. Trust must be given before it's earned. If not, then trusting someone is conditional, which is a slippery slope. I realize for some this is a hard concept to wrap their minds around. If you prove that I can trust you, so be it. But until you do, I will keep my options open. Conditional trust is not a full commitment to a healthy marriage. Marriage is not a 50/50 proposition: You give half and I give half. Marriage is a 100/100 commitment: I will give my all and you give your all. A healthy marriage must have trust at its core. It is the key component to having the marriage of your dreams.

### I Trusted Betty Ann's Faithfulness to Me

There was never a question about Betty Ann's loyalty to me and our marriage. Her fidelity was unquestioned. I never had any doubts about how much she loved me. What she said to me backed up what she did for me. That was so freeing.

Even though we both had been married before, we never once called each other by the name of our former spouses, even during sensitive moments. That always amazed us. Why? Because for the first time in our lives, we were spending life with someone who wanted to spend life with us. Faithfulness begat faithfulness.

There were no emotional walls between us. There was nothing in our lives that we kept hidden from one another. When we were engaged in a deep conversation about something that would affect both of us, I would say to her in Spanish *Mi vida es tu vida* (my life is your life). We knew each other's deepest and darkest secrets. There was nothing in our pasts that we did not know about each other. This created an atmosphere where there was never a concern about someone being unfaithful. When there is no fear of unfaithfulness ever raising its ugly head, you can love with full abandon.

Every time she told me she loved me you could hear the sincerity in her voice. This did not happen once or twice a day; she said it often, seven days a week. There was no pretense. She meant it. Most of the time she gave me the hand sign for *I love you*.

### I Trusted Betty Ann's Confidence in Me

No one, and I mean no one, ever had more confidence in me than my sweet Betty Ann. The girl believed I could do anything

I set my mind to. This was so freeing. It released me to pursue things that were only dreams before. Honestly, some dreams turned out to be nightmares. But she never lost confidence in me when that happened. She was always my biggest supporter and defender.

Her unshakable confidence in me began to produce some really good dividends. With her unwavering support, I became more cautious when I considered chasing after an idea. When someone you love has total confidence in you, you are more likely to pump the breaks when making a decision that will not only affect you but your spouse as well. The belief and confidence your spouse have in you create a willingness to pray more about the opportunities that you may be considering. I am absolutely convinced that the victories I was able to achieve are to be contributed to the confidence Betty Ann had in me. She was my biggest fan, always cheering me on.

When Holy Spirit tugged on my heart strings to start writing, I was reluctant. The only thing I knew about writing was that it consumes a lot of your time and requires a lot of emotional energy. I discussed with Betty Ann what I felt God was saying to me and that I needed her prayer support. I received nothing but her wholehearted allegiance. She told me God had deposited a lot of spiritual truth in me over the last fifty years and that I really needed to seriously consider being obedient to what I felt He was saying to me.

So I sat down one day and started writing. I was amazed how things began to flow. I knew the Holy Spirit was working in and through me. Writing became my passion. Instead of spending my free time with horses and playing golf, I spent it writing.

One day we were talking about how much life I was getting from writing, and she said, "I told you. God has sown into you for years, Wayne, and now He is drawing it out of your soul, so it can be sown in others."

My sweet convent partner had confidence in me when I doubted myself. A lot can be accomplished when someone believes in you.

## *I Trusted Betty Ann's Honesty with Me*

Early in our relationship, I thought it was a good idea for Betty Ann to be added to my checking account. If something were to happen to me, she would have access to the account. She had the authority to write checks or withdraw funds as needed. When we first added her name, I am not sure she really thought I was serious. I had trusted her with the baggage of my past, so why would I not trust her with my checkbook?

After a short time she received a bill that she did not have the funds to pay. Feeling the pressure, she wrote a check out of my (our) account. Unfounded gilt falsely accused her of being untrustworthy. The enemy tried to put her under condemnation by his lies. She felt that what she did might cause me to lose confidence in her. The enemy had convinced her that I would get angry and remove her name from my account. She actually thought I might reject her.

She needed to get this off of her chest, so she called her sister for counsel. Her sister told her that she really needed to tell me about it. And she did. I will never forget the look of self-condemnation on her face when she said she needed to talk to me about something she had done. I listened as she opened up her heart to me. Tears of contrition flowed down her cheeks as she confessed. That made me love her more than ever. I knew I could trust her.

You can't believe the relief that flooded over her when I said, "The banking account belongs to you, too. You have just as much right to the funds as I do."

She grabbed me and squeezed so tight I thought I was going to have to yell, "Calf rope." That was the moment Betty Ann's trust was validated. I knew the Lord had given me someone special. During the twenty-one years we were married, we never had a trust issue. I can't tell you how liberating it is to know your spouse will not keep anything from you. She was always honest with me. Always.

## I Trusted Betty Ann's Counsel to Me

Betty Ann was gifted with a quiet spirit. She was always quick to hear but slow to speak. Her spirit was sensitive, and she was always aware of what was going on around us. People said she could read you like a cheap novel. And she could.

I cannot tell you how many times her sensitive spirit was able to pick up on things that I was totally oblivious to. Her gift kept me out of hot water more times that I can count. I remember on one occasion her telling me I needed to be careful about how I was trusting a certain individual. I really felt she had missed it this time. But she hadn't. Time proved she was right. When I asked her how she knew, she said, "I just knew." From that point on, when she told me to be on guard about something or someone I knew, she knew. Betty Ann always had my best interest at heart.

One day I received an email from someone I know well and love deeply. It was an in-your-face correspondence. This person basically told me to stay out of his life. I was no longer welcome or needed. It was extremely painful, to say the least. I kept that email for a long time, reading it occasionally. Every time I did, painful memories and hurt resurfaced.

One day I mentioned to Betty Ann how I experienced moments of depression every time I read it. She listened without saying a word, allowing me to vent.

When I got through regurgitating all my negative feelings, she said, "Cowboy, you have a big, loving heart. Loving hearts are easily hurt or broken. Every time you read that email, it puts you in the mulligrubs. Have you ever thought about discarding it?"

My sweet wife did not tell me to throw it away. She gave me wise counsel. I knew she was right, so I wadded it into a ball and threw it into the trash. I felt an immediate release. I would love to say this person and I reconciled our differences, but we never have. But I did trust Betty Ann's counsel.

I had confidence in her, because I knew she was always thinking about me. She always had my best interest at heart. This precious soulmate of mine wanted nothing but the best for me. She never told me what to do in any given situation. Never. She laid out the different options that were available and then let me decide what I was going to do. And she never chided me if I made the wrong choice. How can you not trust the counsel of someone like that?

## I Trusted Betty Ann's Love for Me

I've always been taught that assumption is the lowest form of knowledge. We can assume something is right even though we don't have any proof. The longer I live, the more I agree with that claim.

Take love for example. Most people assume love is primarily feelings. As long as you have good vibes and feelings about someone or something, everything is copacetic. Have you noticed how our feelings ebb and flow? Our feelings constantly fluctuate. This is why people say things like, "I just don't love them anymore," or "We have fallen out of love." Most people, believers and unbelievers alike, allow their feelings and emotions to dictate whether they are in love. This makes our commitment to love our spouses until death parts us conditional. As long as we feel we are in love, we're good to go. But if our feelings tell us we are no longer in love, escape becomes an option. It makes it easier to cut the cords of our marriage covenants.

Love is not defined by feelings. That is a hard pill for most people to swallow. It was for me when I first received this revelation. It is hard to wrap our minds around that truth because we live in a society that is driven by feelings and emotions. If you don't believe that, pay attention to the next commercial you see or hear. Let me make a quick disclaimer. I am not saying feelings are unimportant and have no place in our relationships. What I am saying is that we may not have a healthy understanding of what love really means.

## Four Kinds of Biblical Love

The word love is tossed around a lot in our culture. We love a good movie, just like we love good food. We love good food just like we love our pets. We love our pets just like we love our families. The word love is used to describe our feelings about someone or something, not realizing that there is a difference between loving your spouse and loving a good round of golf. We could spend the rest of our lives talking about what we love. Because many words in the English language are so abstract at times, our natural tendency is to use the same word to define many things.

When we use the word love, most if not all the time, we are talking about our feelings, how we feel about something. This is not true in biblical language. Words are very specific and descriptive. Take the word *love* as an example. There are four words for love in the New Testament. Each word is specifically used to differentiate the difference in what kind of love is being expressed. Is it family love, brotherly love, romantic love, or godly love?

The Greek word *eros* is used to define sensual or romantic love that should be guarded and protected within the marriage union. The word *philia* speaks to brotherly love, or deep friendship. (Philadelphia is known as the city of brotherly love.) Sometimes the word *storge* will be used to describe family love. Then we have the word *agape,* the kind of love our heavenly Father has for us. It is the kind of love that should exist between a husband and wife. The Word of God admonishes husbands to love their wives as Christ loved the church (Ephesians 5:25).

What is so interesting about *agape* is that it is not based on feelings. It is loving someone out of one's will. God doesn't love us because we make Him feel good. He loves us out of His nature. He is love (1 John 4:8). This makes it possible for Him to love us when we are lovable, but more importantly, He loves us when we are unlovable. This messes with a lot of people's theology.

What about feelings? Are they not important? Feelings will be present but do not determine our commitments to our soulmates. Loving one's spouse comes from the will. When our feelings and emotions toward our spouses are not where they should be, or where we want them to be, we don't cut the marriage strings and run. Our marriage covenant remains intact. If we allow our emotions to dictate why and how we love, we will be jerked around like a kite in a high wind.

I would feel remiss if I did not state once again what could save your marriage. I will do it in two sentences. When stress encroaches the boundaries of a marriage, feelings may change, but the marriage remains intact because it is held together by our wills, not our feelings. We must make a conscious decision to agape our soulmates regardless of how we feel.

Betty Ann did not love me like she loved liver and onions. Her love was not conditional. She loved me in spite of how I may have acted at times. That's agape. The love she had for me was not based on her feelings and emotions. It is an incredible blessing to be loved by someone who wants to love you, especially your covenant partner. You cannot help but love your partner in return.

# 6

## She Had a Giving Spirit

Love gives. "*For God so loved the world that He gave His only begotten Son*, that whoever believes in Him should not perish but have everlasting life" (John 3:16 NKJV, emphasis added). Our heavenly Father demonstrated to the whole world, past, present, and future, what true love is. True love always gives its best. Always. A giving spirit is a reflection of the indwelling presence of the Father's heart in us.

Betty Ann was the most generous person I have ever met. Because she was an extravagant giver, you had to keep an eye on her because she would give away the kitchen sink. She might even give away the kitchen if you did not stay on your toes. This Proverbs Thirty-Two woman was willing to live in lack if she could help meet someone else's need. I saw her do this time and time again. She was an amazing lady.

Betty Ann never gave anything expecting compensation. An authentic giver never does. It actually never crosses their minds. Their motivation is to bring a little sunshine to someone's gloomy day. And my beloved soulmate did just that.

## A Giving Spirit Reveals a Person's Heart

A generous spirit does not originate from outside us. Giving is a matter of the heart. As a matter of fact, anything we say or do comes from the core of our innermost being. Whatever is on the inside will sooner or later reveal itself. Betty Ann had a generous heart. Everyone who knew her would attest to that.

Jesus spoke the following words to a group of self-righteous Pharisees who were accusing Him of being the devil's pawn. "You brood of snakes! How could evil men like you speak what is good and right? *For whatever is in your heart determines what you say*" (Matthew 12:34 NLT, emphasis added). What we say with our mouths is who we really are. This same principle can be applied to giving. A giving spirit reveals a person's heart.

Three months after Betty Ann went to be with Jesus, I mustered up enough emotional energy to start the process of going through her personal belongings. I found gifts tucked away in inconspicuous places that she had bought for people but never had the opportunity to give them. It reminded me again of something I already knew: She was a highly generous soul. What she left behind still lives on.

## A Giving Spirit Is an Expression of Love

No one on this earth, and I mean no one, has ever loved me like my Proverbs Thirty-Two woman. With the spirit of John 3:16 in her soul, she *so loved me* that she always gave me her best, no matter what it was or how she felt.

At Christmastime she was a hoot to watch. She was usually the last one to open her gifts because she was so focused on watching people open the ones she had given them. She always had a smile on her face, too. When someone opened one of her gifts, she would say something like, "I remember you saying you needed one of these," or "You told me you wanted one like that." Christmas in our home was a history maker. I love Christmas, but I have to admit I am thankful that it comes around only once a year. I'll bet you can guess why.

She always gave the best gifts. She never gave the generic version of anything. It had to be the name brand. I really believe she was more excited about giving than the person was who received them. This is typical of someone with a giving spirit.

Throughout the year it was common for her to give me a gift that she called a JB gift: *just because*. The gift wasn't for my birthday, anniversary, Christmas, or any other special occasion. It was just because she loved me. The gift would have a love note attached to it with the letters JB. Just because.

## A Giving Spirit Has a Testimony

I heard a testimony years ago that the Holy Spirit had used to give me a revelation about giving. I will never forget it. It happened at a mission banquet I was attending. Several missionaries were there to talk about their ministries and what God was doing in their particular mission field. At this banquet I heard a testimony that tremendously impacted my life. It did not come from the podium by a missionary but was shared by a lady sitting with her husband at my table.

There was a lot of chatter and laughter going on before the conference began. With four couples assigned to each table, you can imagine the noise that was being made by eight people who were enjoying their time together. During the random conversations, someone asked one of the ladies sitting at our table how her mother was doing. It is sad to say I can't tell you anything the missionaries had to say, but I can recite every word this lady told us about her mother.

Her aging mother had been having some serious health issues. She had felt it was time for her to give away some of her personal belongs to her children. This way her kids would probably get what they wanted that would keep their mother's memory alive and fresh. It would also save any hassle that might take place over her material possessions after she had passed on. Over a period of two years, she had given most of her belongings to her kids

Then it happened: Her home caught fire and burned to the ground. Everything she owned was destroyed. Her kids responded immediately to take care of their mother. They tried to give back all the possessions she had given them. What she said is what has stuck with me all these years. She told them the only thing she had left was what she had given away. Let that sink in for a moment. The only thing we really have is what we have given away.

Betty Ann left a lot behind when she made her transition from earth to heaven. What she left will continue to live on. And it is not the gifts she gave to people over the years but the memories people have of her generosity, knowing they were in her thoughts and prayers. Her heart and generous spirit still speak and will continue to speak for a long, long time.

## A Giving Spirit Has a Voice

Our heavenly Father can hear a generous heart. That may sound a little weird to some. Our giving speaks? Yes, a giving spirit has a voice. We may not be able to hear it, but our heavenly Father sure does.

Here is something worth filing away in your memory bank. The size of one's gift is not what determines how big it is. The size of one's gift is what a person has left after he or she has given. Jesus taught this.

> Now Jesus sat opposite the treasury and saw how the people put money into the treasury. And many who were rich put in much. Then one poor widow came and threw in two mites, which make a quadrans. So He called His disciples to Himself and said to them, "*Assuredly, I say to you that this poor widow has put in more than all those who have given to the treasury, for they all put in out of their abundance, but she out of her poverty put in all that she had, her whole livelihood.*" (Mark 12:41–44 NKJV, emphasis added)

Why in the world would Jesus say something like that about the widow's gift? It is obvious to our natural reasoning that her gift could not compare to what the wealthy people were giving. And Jesus said that she gave more than anyone. She gave two mites, for crying out loud. What did she have left after giving? Not one thing. She had given all she had. And Jesus said she gave more than anyone. The sound of her heart was in her gift, and Jesus heard it.

That reminds me so much of my Betty Ann, my Proverbs Thirty-Two woman. She had a giving spirit and was the most generous giver I have ever known in my life, bar none. She gave all, all the time.

## A Giving Spirit Is Always Focused on Others

Being generous to others is a fundamental principle of Christian spirituality. Giving is what determines the harvest.

Remember this: A farmer who plants only a few seeds will get a small crop. But the one who plants generously will get a generous crop. You must each decide in your heart how much to give. And don't give reluctantly or in response to pressure. "For God loves a person who gives cheerfully." And God will generously provide all you need. Then you will always have everything you need and plenty left over to share with others. (2 Corinthians 9:6–8 NLT).

Paul says in verse 10 of this same passage, "For God is the one who provides seed for the farmer and then bread to eat. In the same way, he will provide and increase your resources and then produce a great harvest of generosity in you." I think you would be blessed if you were to read the entire chapter of 2 Corinthians on giving. God allows us to set the measurement for our receiving, and it's by our giving. This may seem counterintuitive, but it is the economy of the kingdom.

B. A. was liberal in her giving to others, even during times we were financially challenged. But God always provided for us during these seasons. I am convinced He did because of my generous wife. She never placed giving to others on the back burner. People with needs always got her undivided attention. She was a woman who had a giving spirit.

## Betty Ann Always Put Me First

I never had to wonder where I was on her list of priorities. When it came to her business, our children and grandchildren, or anything else, she always kept me at the top of her list. By no means does that mean she was not committed to making sure her boutique was a success, or that she did not love our kids and grandkids. They were always on her mind and in her heart. But Betty Ann believed the Word of God was true and did her best to live it out in her daily life. Genesis 2:24 was the scripture we both committed our lives to when we got married. "This explains why a man leaves his father and mother and *is joined to his wife, and the two are united into one*" (NLT, emphasis added).

Marriages can get into serious trouble if either or both parties try to become one with anything or anyone other than their spouse, saying things like, "My kids are the most important things in my life," and "There's nothing I wouldn't do for my kids."

These words, and others like them, are said by people who do not understand the marriage covenant. As a matter of fact, we do untold harm to our children when we make them more important to us than the ones we are married to. If we would do what the Word of God tells us, we would have a deeper and healthier relationship with our children. And our spouses would always be number one in our lives. This would demonstrate to our children how they are to treat their spouses when they leave home and get married.

The way Betty Ann treated me created a desire to make her my number-one priority. She was at the top of my favorite list. If you wanted to see the bad side of me, just say something about my wife, or mistreat her in any way. If you find this hard to believe, just ask our girls.

Making your spouse number one is the tool a healthy and vibrant marriage must have to become all that God has designed it to be. It pays great dividends.

### *She Gave Me Respect and Honor*

If there is anything a person needs more than anything else, it is respect and honor. Betty Ann never demeaned me in any way. She never said anything derogatory about me in front of anyone, especially family members. My Proverbs Thirty-Two woman never showed disrespect for me in private either. She always gave me respect and honor. That was her spirit.

I cannot count how many times I said to her, "I'm so glad you have a low benchmark."

All she would do is grin and say, "I'm glad you're mine."

She made it so easy for me to love her.

As former NFL player Reggie Brooks said, "To give honor and respect is the best way for a marriage to get to the destination of 'together forever.'" Amen!

People need to be respected and honored in private, but even more so in public. She never corrected me in public, even when I needed correction. Love, honor, and respect are what make a marriage indestructible. Feelings are not fundamental to love, honor, and respect; they are the fruits of loving, honoring, and respecting your covenant partner.

## She Gave Me Permission to Fail

Nothing can damage or destroy a person more than failing. Our tendency is to see ourselves based on performance. If we fail, we must be failures. I don't think there is anyone who enjoys coming out on the bottom of the pile—no sane person, anyway.

Talking about our victories and successes is not a problem for most of us. Sharing our failures is another story. To have the freedom to share our losses, we must have a safe place, a place where we will be loved unconditionally no matter what. It is amazing what you can accomplish when you know that the one you love has your back. My beloved provided that safe place for me.

I must give credit where credit is due. Betty Ann deserves all the credit for the things I have been able to accomplish, especially in my senior years. She was always my biggest fan. I never had to concern myself with whether she was in my corner or not. Knowing she was gave me incredible confidence in whatever I was doing, because I knew that if things did not work out like I had planned, she would not deride or ridicule me. That was so freeing. Because she gave me permission to fail, she freed me to pursue my dreams. I've never had anyone give me their wholehearted support in whatever I attempted to do like Betty Ann.

"You can do this," she would say. And those words spurred me on to succeed more than I failed.

## *She Gave Me the Kind of Marriage You Dream About*

I am serious when I say this: I wish every married couple could have what Betty Ann and I had. A lot of couples do, but far too many don't. Every day was a good day for us. We would take a bad day and make it a good day on purpose. That is the choice we chose to make. In no way am I insinuating that every day was bright and sunny. We went through some stormy days together. Life can be unfair at times, but God did not say it wouldn't be. We refused to allow the situations and circumstances we found ourselves in to affect the covenant we made to one another. This is a choice every couple has to make. It is a decision that must be based on our will, not on feelings. If we allow our feelings and emotions to have the steering wheel of our lives, we will be in love one day and not the next. Feelings are schizophrenic.

Our home was a place we loved to run to, not away from. It was a place you felt safe and protected. We loved being together. Betty Ann spent a lot of time with me at horse sales. And it wasn't because she loved horses that much. She knew I did and wanted to be with me. I spent a lot of time in the women's shoe department at Dillard's, and not because I was infatuated by women's shoes. I enjoyed being with my Proverbs -Thirty-Two woman.

We knew if we kept the Lord as our number-one priority, individually and collectively, we would have a peaceful and healthy marriage, a marriage the devil could not destroy. And this we did. The Lord Jesus Christ was our number-one topic of discussion. We worshipped together, took communion in our home on a regular basis, prayed together, and discussed what we felt the Lord was saying to us. We understood that He is our lives (Acts 17:28).

I can say this about Betty Ann without reservation. She found her home in the Word of God. She chose the faith book over Facebook. When people share testimonies about Betty Ann, they always mention how much time they saw her reading the Bible. What they saw her doing in public, I saw her doing at home. This was no facade. She was legit.

The girl could prepare some good food. I don't think there was anything she could not cook. Everyone loved to eat Betty Ann's cooking. At get-togethers where food was served, it was not uncommon to hear someone say, "Betty Ann, what did you bring?" When I loaded my plate, the first dish I dipped out of was whatever she made. We always took home an empty dish, too. Some were so clean we didn't have to wash them. Just kidding on the wash part.

The last couple of years of her life, the cooking responsibilities were handed off to me. That was unsettling because I could not boil water. She could make boiled water taste good. Cooking was not even on my dislike list. But things changed. Everything I know now about cooking Betty Ann taught me. She did not have a good student in me, but I had one incredible teacher. I started to enjoy cooking, and my culinary skills have improved.

The stovetop was not more than twenty feet from where she lay. Even in her uncomfortable state of health, she would walk me through the process of whatever I was cooking.

After we ate, she would say, "You're a good little cooker. I just may keep you for one more week."

My sweet wife lived her life for me. It did not matter what it was, she made sure I was first in order. She did this for twenty-one years without a hiccup. My clothes got laundered before anyone else's. My plate was the first one she filled and served. I never had a need she did not take care of. And she always did it with a smile. Betty Ann was the epitome of what a good soulmate should be. She understood that living her life for others was the only way she could make an eternal investment that would pay huge dividends.

We enjoyed talking to one another. There is something soothing about hearing the voice of the one you love and are in covenant with. It did not matter where I was, in the country or out, we talked every day. We did not allow distance to keep us from telling each other that we loved them.

One of the most memorable conversations we had was when I was on the Maasai Mara National Reserve in Kenya, Africa. I was sitting in a chair watching the stars twinkle in the African sky. We heard the sounds of wild animals all around us. And there I was, talking to the love of my life on my cell phone as if she were in a chair next to me. This is one memory I will always cherish. She told me how proud she was of me for being obedient to what the Lord had assigned me to do.

After our long conversation she said, "I love you, Cowboy. I can't wait till you get home."

She is now in the presence of her Lord and Savior, Jesus Christ, the One she had given her life to and lived her life for. I can imagine her saying, "Cowboy, I can't wait till you come home. You're not going to believe this place."

My beloved Betty Ann had a giving spirit. She knew the only thing she had was what she had given away. And she gave it all.

# 7

*She Believed in Me*

IT IS AMAZING WHAT YOU CAN ACCOMPLISH WHEN SOMEONE believes in you, especially when that person is your covenant partner.

What Betty Ann said to me while she sat on the tailgate of my truck the day I emptied all the closets of my life to her, she meant it: "Wayne, you're a good man."

She did not know it at the time, but those were words I desperately needed to hear. Betty Ann wanted me to believe in myself. My fear of failure began to subside. My confidence level started rising. Her words created a desire to be the kind of person she believed I was. Everything I have been able to accomplish in my life and ministry is because my beautiful wife had confidence in me.

Betty Ann saw in me what I could not see. Not only did she see it, she was continuously calling it out. She was not just my biggest fan, she was my personal motivational coach. No matter what I was going through, she always gave me wise counsel, and a thumbs-up sign: You can do this. She gave me some incredible insights into living life: You never lose. You either win or learn, but you never lose. How good is that?

## She Kept Me Focused on My Strengths

It's human nature to focus on weaknesses. If we fall victim to this, it will keep us from seeing our strengths or from ever tapping into our potential. Our time will be consumed with trying to become what Christ has already made us to be. When this happens, performance will take center stage in our lives.

This is why it is so important to have someone in our corners who is committed to cheering us on. Someone who believes in us. No one can fill this place better than a committed soulmate. Count yourself blessed if your spouse is your biggest encourager. B. A. was mine. She kept me focused on my strengths and possibilities.

As I said earlier, I was labeled a dreamer by those who played a significant role in my nurturing years. I was told that so often that I believed they were right: I was just a dreamer with no substance. Dreaming kept me detached from reality. I am convinced those who called me a dreamer did not do so because they wanted to see me fail in life. It was done out of ignorance. If you don't know, you don't know.

Betty Ann helped me come to understand that I was not just a dreamer. I was not living in a world consisting of only dreams. I was a visionary. God had gifted me with the ability to see the possibilities of what could be accomplished if I only had someone to believe in me. God gifted me with that someone: my Proverbs Thirty-Two woman.

I have a deep affinity to what the writer of Proverbs meant when he wrote

> Her children stand and bless her. *Her husband praises her;* there are many virtuous and capable women in the world, but you surpass them all! Charm is deceptive, and beauty does not last, but a woman who fears the Lord will be greatly praised. Reward her for all she has done. *Let her deeds publicly declare her praise.* (Proverbs 31:28–31 NLT, emphasis added)

I do praise her today for keeping me focused on my strengths and not allowing what others may say or think keep me from pursuing the visions God has planted in my spirit.

## She Encouraged Me to Keep Pursuing My Dreams

I remember when the Holy Spirit began to download into me the revelation about our new creation identities as children of God, that we are more than sinners saved by grace. We are new creations in Christ, old things have passed away, and all things are now new, just like the Word of God says (2 Corinthians 5:17). It has been an eye opener. The Spirit of God opened up the scriptures like I had never seen them before. It brought incredible peace to my life and took my love for my heavenly Father to a new level.

Here is what He showed me. My identity as a child of God is not based on performance. It is not based on what I have to do to be in right standing with Him. It is all about what He has done for me. He (Christ) was made what I was so I could be like He is (2 Corinthians 5:21).

One day, Betty Ann and I were talking about the revelation of identity the Lord was bringing to His people. She told me doors of opportunities were going to open for me to share this message. It would be doors much larger than I had envisioned. Others were telling me the same thing, but their words did not carry the same weight as my beloved's. She believed in me. I knew I had her full support.

Those doors she talked about did begin to open: Did they ever. I am not a huge fan of traveling, especially out of country. But these opened doors took me to places I never saw myself sharing the message of our new creation identities. We had prayed for this opportunity, and God was answering our prayers. Before I knew it, I was spending a considerable amount of time in other countries teaching and preaching this message. Sometimes these trips were for an extended period of time. Not one time did she complain about me being away. She was excited that I was being given the privilege to share what the Lord had shown me.

One return trip from Africa will be forever etched in my mind. I got home at midnight from a trip to Uganda where we saw God do some extraordinary things. Standing at the door to greet me were my sweet wife and our youngest daughter, Alex. Betty Ann was holding an eight-week-old puppy in her arms. One day I had casually mentioned that I was thinking about getting a lab puppy to train for pheasant hunting. If I ever did, it would be given the name Duggan, named after a dear pastor friend and fellow pheasant hunter.

Meeting me at the front door at that hour in the morning with a big smile on her face, she gave me a kiss and a firm hug and then she handed me the puppy. "We would like for you to meet Duggan."

No matter what was going on, I was always number one in my beloved's heart. I never had to wonder where I was on her list of priorities.

## *She Encouraged Me to Write*

One day, Betty Ann suggested I should pray about putting the revelation about identity the Lord had given me in book form. I really did not see that happening. Writing was not something that came easily for me. In the back recesses of my mind, I thought about writing a book, but it never seemed the time was right. Maybe I would someday. But she never wavered in her confidence that I could.

Betty Ann had been battling cancer for five years when she firmly began to encourage me to start writing. Her weakened condition would not allow her to sleep in our bed because it was too high and she ran the risk of falling. So we made her a comfortable spot on the couch in the living area close to the kitchen. Because she needed constant attention, I set up my computer at the kitchen table so I could hear her if she needed anything. This also gave us the ability to talk to each other during the day. Even though she did not feel well, she never stopped encouraging me to write. Her thoughts were always on me, even when she felt horrible.

"I will give it a try," I said to myself on this particular morning when I sat down at my computer. *I know the new creation identity is in my heart; I will see if it will make its way through my fingertips when I start typing.*

So I started. The Lord allowed Betty Ann to be with me for another year and a half. During this time, the Spirit of God helped me write eleven books. Several have already been published, with more in the process of being published.

During this short period, Betty Ann continued to get weaker, which made it difficult for her to focus on anything for any length of time. Her immune system was incredibly compromised by 109 chemo treatments. In addition to that, her body had been radiated twenty times. She never had the chance or the strength to read any of the books I've written, but she kept encouraging me to write.

She told me, "I really don't have to read them, Cowboy. I hear them coming out of your heart every day, and have for years. Glad you're mine."

She believed in me and never stopped encouraging me to write. This is why I am writing this book, *My Proverbs Thirty-Two Woman*. And I'm writing it from my kitchen table. The sad thing is I can't turn around and tell her what the Holy Spirit has given me. And I have found myself doing that on many occasions. Those are sobering moments. I may no longer be able to see Betty Ann with my eyes on this side of eternity, but I can feel her in my heart every day. I am so thankful she kept believing in me even when I did not believe in myself.

## She Encouraged Me to Never Give Up

When I made the move from East Texas to the Texas Panhandle, I really believed that after twenty-seven years my pastoring season was over. That was heart-wrenching because pastoring is what gives me life. I have never regretted one day of being in the ministry. Oh, there are some challenging times that all ministers go through. No pastor is immune from that fact. But the good always outweighs the bad. To be honest, I can't remember most of the bad times because they are absorbed by the good ones.

I had no idea what was ahead of me when I made my move to a part of Texas, I had told myself I would never live. I did not have a clue that as the doors behind me were closing, God was opening up new ones I never knew existed. What appeared to be the ending was actually the beginning.

My love for the Lord never waned, and the joy I got from preaching never went away. There was no doubt whatsoever in my mind that God had called me to preach. I just felt my pastoring days were over, which saddened my heart.

Over the years I had been critical and judgmental of pastors who are divorced. Now, I found myself in the same situation. I am one of them. I can give personal testimony to the fact that a large segment of the community of faith does hold divorced pastors in contempt. Praise God that His gifts and calling are irrevocable (Romans 11:29).

One day, Betty Ann listened to me opine about what I thought I had lost, regurgitating my feelings and emotions. It was nasty.

When I finished venting, she said, "Whatever you do, Wayne, please don't give up."

Quitting or giving up was never on my radar, but I desperately needed to hear some encouraging words.

I had been in the Texas Panhandle for about two weeks when I participated in a roping clinic held at a barn church's arena. It was a lot of fun, and as usual, I was being a clown. I do enjoy making people laugh.

When we broke for lunch, the PBR roper who was teaching this clinic said to me, "What is your story?"

I spent about fifteen minutes sharing my testimony. When we finished lunch and were headed back to rope some more, an individual who was listening to my testimony asked if I would be willing to come to his church and share it. Of course, I said yes. That testimony given at a roping clinic was the door God used to keep me in the preaching saddle. From that day to the present, I have not missed one week of sharing my heart, and it has been twenty-three years. I am finishing my race the way it began—preaching the Word of God.

The leadership of the church where I serve as senior pastor had visited with me on several occasions to see if I would be interested in becoming their pastor. My answer was always no. This did not keep them from pursuing me. I really did not want to be their pastor because I was having so much fun being an itinerant preacher/teacher. Finally, I made a commitment to pray about it, as did the church leadership. Betty Ann was also praying for me to know the will of God.

After several weeks praying about this, I felt in my heart that I should accept the offer the church had extended. I bounced this off Betty Ann. She told me that she thought I was their man. I told her I did too but did not want to be.

Before I accepted their invitation, I had a serious conversation with Betty Ann about it. I told her I was going to say yes. Then I told her that if things ever got too difficult, just tell me and I will walk away in a heartbeat.

She said, "You would do that for me?"

Knowing she would be my first priority kept us both free.

One day Betty Ann and I were driving back from a preaching engagement at a rodeo event.

During our discussion about how good God is, she said, "I'm glad you never gave up, Cowboy. You make me so proud."

I am not sure anyone could be more thankful than me for not giving in to the enemy's lies and walking away from ministry. Betty Ann's encouragement kept me moving ahead even when there was no light for me to see where I was going. We do have to walk by faith.

Once a person gives up on anything, it makes is so much easier to give up on other things. Betty Ann was going to make sure that did not happen to me. She was always an encourager because she believed in me.

## *She Encouraged Me to Keep the Doors of My Heart and Home open to My Adult Children*

The breakup of a marriage does not only affect the man and the woman, it usually causes collateral damage as well. It affects the kids too, regardless of their age. That can be as painful, if not more so, than the divorce itself. They feel pain in ways parents cannot know. It threatens their emotional security. In many cases the children never totally recover. The pain they feel is stuffed down inside them, and if it never gets dealt with, their pain becomes a vindictive spirit that keeps them tethered to their hurts.

I lost all credibility with my kids when their mother and I divorced. They were aware of the trouble that existed in our home for a long time. It was no secret. But here is the raw truth: kids would rather their parents stay together and be miserable than to be free and happy apart. There are exceptions of course, and I can understand that. I would be a little concerned if this were not the case. Even though a marriage may be on the verge of collapsing, most children want their parents to remain together. There is something about family unity that resides deep within us, and when that unity is threatened, the results can be devastating to everyone involved.

One day I was sharing with Betty Ann the pain I felt about my broken relationship with my kids. She patiently let me vent.

When I was through, she said, "I know you, and if there was any way you could restore your relationship with your kids, you would. Until that happens, keep the doors of your heart and our home open to them. I believe it will happen in time."

Because my son's sweet wife kept encouraging him to reestablish our relationship, it happened. I am so proud of the man he has become—husband, father, and teacher/coach. He is a remarkable man. I will forever be grateful to my daughter-in-law for what she did to see that my son and I were reconciled.

I am so thankful that I kept my heart and home open to him, as Betty Ann encouraged me to do. We may actually be closer now than we have ever been. We talk often. He is a man strong in faith who loves his family dearly.

### *My Proverbs Thirty-Two Woman Believed in Me*

When someone believes in you, there is not much you can't accomplish. It not only gives you a sense of purpose, it imparts confidence in you to fulfill that purpose. I never had to wonder if B. A. had my back. Knowing that kept me going when the road got rocky and it looked like I may have made a bad choice. She taught me that sometimes roadblocks serve as tour guides. It may appear that we are being impeded from reaching our goal, but it's the opposite. Roadblocks and detour signs may be there to help us stay on the right path, so that we will see our hopes and dreams come true.

Betty Ann was one of the most intelligent individuals I have ever known. And it's not because her ACT and SAT scores were extremely high. She had what is so conspicuous by its absence today—common sense. She never flaunted it, either. Betty Ann was not quick to give her opinion about anything. We had this conversation many times about her reluctance to share what she thought about something that was under discussion. She told me that if you speak too quickly, you might say something you wish you hadn't, and if you do, it is impossible to take back what you said. She may have been insinuating that I should do the same.

I have never been reluctant to share my opinion. Someone once told me that the only time I opened my mouth was to insert my other foot. To this day I don't have a clue why he would have said such a thing. Well, on second thought ... I do have the tendency to overthink things. In doing so, I can complicate something simple. Betty Ann had a way of untangling the suppositions that were created by my over-scrutinizing something by using common sense. I was guilty of trying to make sense out of nonsense. Her counsel could take the *non* out of *sense,* leaving me with common sense.

Have you noticed the older we get the easier it is for us to focus on our weaknesses to the point where we cannot see our strengths? Failures seem to dominate our thought lives. When this happens, our self-confidence packs its bags and goes on vacation, and sometimes it never returns. All it takes for us to reassign our focus is to have someone who has our best interests at heart, who will call out our giftings and potential. Everyone benefits greatly from having someone who believes in them. So much potential goes dormant, visions become only dreams, giftings are rewrapped in forgetfulness, and we take all our could-have-beens to the graves with us. The epitaph chiseled on most headstones could read something like: "I told you I had a dream."

Faith and fear basically share the same definition. Both believe something is going to happen. Fear believes what happens will be bad. Faith believes it will be good. Betty Ann believed in me. She constantly pointed out my strengths until my fear of failing was pushed out by faith, like light drives out darkness. She changed my life for the better, forever. I am not the same guy I was when she told me that night in my office that she was in love with me. And it was all because she believed in me.

## The Oneness of Marriage

Marriage is more than being in a relationship with someone. A relationship defines dating, and union defines marriage. Marriage is a union of body, soul, and spirit that expresses God's nature. Here is what Proverbs says about a oneness marriage: "Through *wisdom* a house is *built*, and by *understanding* it is *established*, by *knowledge* the rooms are *filled* with all precious and pleasant riches" (Proverbs 24:3–4 NKJV, emphasis added). Did you notice what King Solomon said about a healthy home? It is a home filled with precious and pleasant riches because it has been built with the right building materials: wisdom, understanding, and knowledge. If we attempt to build our homes on anything other than what the Word of God says, we may stay in relationship, but we will never experience the oneness God designed for a man and a woman.

Slowly read the following verses that Paul pined to the church in Corinth, and as you read them, keep what has just been said in mind.

> For we are God's fellow workers, you are God's field, *you are God's building.* According to the grace of God which was given to me, as a wise master builder I have laid the foundation, and another builds on it. *But let each one take heed how he builds on it. For no other foundation can anyone lay than that which is laid, which is Jesus Christ.* (1 Corinthians 3:9–11 NKJV, emphasis added)

Not only must we use the proper materials when building our marriages, we must make certain that we build on the right foundation. This foundation is the Lord Jesus Christ. All other foundations will not be able to withstand the weight life can lay on us.

# 8

## *She Was a Woman Quick to Forgive*

I MAY FORGIVE THEM FOR WHAT THEY DID TO ME, BUT I WILL never forget. Have you ever heard someone say that, or something close to it? Maybe you have even said it yourself. If not, the chances are good there have been times when you thought it. Those words come from deep wounds that have been inflicted upon a person. How can you forget the wrongdoings that were done to you and pretend like they never happened? Forgiveness maybe, but forgetting? That is not going to happen. I may forgive in time, but that will be as far as I can go. Don't ask me to forget. That's not humanly possible.

We all have been wounded at various times in our lives. There's no way to get through life without experiencing hurts. It goes with the territory. It's like death and taxes. It's not if you die, or if you pay taxes, it's when. There is no way to live life unaffected.

## *Forgiving and Forgetting*

There is a big difference between a wound and a scar. Simply put, a scar is a healed wound. A wound will never become a scar until it is healed. How quickly we heal from the hurts and pains that have been inflicted upon us is totally our call (Hebrews 12:12–13). We are in more control of how fast we heal than we may think. Many people are still nursing wounds they received years ago, some as far back as their childhood. We can prolong the healing process if we keep picking at our emotional wounds. The way you pick at a wound is to continually bring it up. That keeps something that happened in the past to remain in our present. It also affects our future.

Forgiveness is not about getting over something, it's about getting through it. And we do that by releasing those who have abused, used, or manipulated us as quickly as possible. As long as we hang on to the hurts someone has perpetrated on us, that person remains in control of our lives. You may be thinking, *No one controls my life.* OK. When was the last time your path was altered because you saw someone you did not want to encounter? Who determined which aisle you took in the grocery store? You know.

It is possible that we may not know what forgiveness really is. Forgiveness is an act of our wills, not our emotions or feelings. If we waited until we felt like forgiving someone, we may never do it. God has given us the ability to change our feelings and emotions by exercising our free wills that He gifted us with, and choose to do what He told us. Forgiving is the only way we can get free and stay free. Unforgiveness keeps us prisoners.

What about forgetting? Is that really possible, or is it simply a religious exercise that will get us through the moment but have no long-term effect on our spiritual health? Just like forgiving, forgetting is an act of our wills, not how we feel. Can we really choose to forget? The answer is a resounding *yes*!

There is nothing that can be hidden from an all-seeing, all-knowing God. He is omniscient. Keep that in mind as you read the following scripture written by the Old Testament prophet Jeremiah. "For I will *forgive* their iniquity, and their sin I will *remember* no more" (Jeremiah 31:34 NKJV, emphasis added).

God forgives and forgets. Read that verse again and allow the Holy Spirit to brand it deep into your soul. I think it's fairly easy for us to embrace the truth that God forgives our iniquities. But this verse also says God will not remember our sins anymore. That immediately causes us to raise our hands and beg the questions: If God knows everything, how can He forget anything? If He does not remember our sins, then how would it be possible for Him to know everything?

That's a legitimate couple of questions to ask. Maybe, just maybe, we don't know what forgetting really means. And by not knowing, it makes sense that we can forgive but not believe we can forget.

Look closely at the word *remember*. God will not remember our sins. Let me tweak this word just a little and see if the light begins to come on: *re*member. Let's say you lost a finger in an accident and were taken to the hospital along with your severed finger. A skilled surgeon may be able to reattach the lost finger to your hand. In other words, the doctor was able to *re*member, or reattach it to its proper place.

God, who is the Great Physician, promised us He would never reattach our sins to us again. That's what it means to forget. He will never mention our sins again. When we forgive and forget, we release the person who inflicted us with pain, and we don't bring up the wrongs that were done to us. We want from God what we are not willing to give to others: Forgiveness and forgetting the wrongs they have done.

## Betty Ann Understood Forgiving and Forgetting

Betty Ann may not have been a seminary graduate, but she understood something about forgiving and forgetting that most people never discover. What I've learned about forgiving and forgetting came from her. It was not just the words she spoke. She gave legs to her words by her actions. It is easy to talk about forgiving and forgetting, but most of the time it is not easy to do. But we must never forget that with God, all things are possible (Matthew 19:26).

To keep unforgiveness from festering and metastasizing, my precious wife made the choice to forgive others a priority. As quickly as possible, we need to forgive and release the people who have inflicted us with pain and hurt. The quicker we do this, the better it is for us.

Betty Ann looked to Jesus as her example. "Then Jesus said, 'Father, forgive them, for they do not know what they do'" (Luke 23:34 NKJV). Just in case you need to be reminded, these words were spoken by Jesus when he was hanging on the cross dying for you and me. Forgiving and forgetting is a choice.

What an example Betty Ann was to me and to those who knew her. "Who can find a virtuous wife? For her worth is far above rubies. The heart of her husband safely trusts her" (Proverbs 31:10–11 NKJV). That's a Proverbs Thirty-Two woman.

## Betty Ann Forgave because She Knew She Was Forgiven

Betty Ann had some unpleasant things happen when she was growing up that continued into her early adult life. There were some awful things said about her and done to her. But I never knew her to carry a grudge. She refused to allow the people who hurt her to live in her mind rent-free. She did not like drama and avoided it at all costs.

My mother passed away not long after Betty Ann and I were married. It was a reality check for all of us grown kids. Things are not the same without your mother. Betty Ann's love and support made a difficult moment so much easier. I shared this earlier but it's worth repeating. At the memorial service, one of my family members said something vile and nefarious about Betty Ann. And it was said so she could hear. It takes an evil heart to say what this person said, especially at such an emotional and sensitive time. Betty Ann never responded. It brought tears to my eyes when she told me what this person said.

I will never forget what she told me when we were discussing what had happened. "This individual has a lot of pain, shame, and unforgiveness in her heart. What she said came out of the deep hidden recesses of her innermost being. Her words revealed who she really is. Most people see this person one way, but the words this person said revealed who she really is."

What we say does reveal what is in our hearts, and an exposed heart reveals our true character (Luke 6:43–45). Betty Ann told me she would not hold what this individual said against her. Talk about class. My sweetheart was one classy lady. She chose to forgive this person because she knew God had forgiven her. She forgave as she was forgiven. Her example created in me a desire to release and let go of some people. That is the only way to experience true freedom.

## Old Covenant Forgiveness verses New Covenant Forgiveness

We could define covenant this way: It is how God deals with people. That is a simple but very efficient definition. It is how God interacts with humanity. The old covenant is how He once dealt with humanity, and the new covenant is how He deals with humanity now. Under the law, you forgave in order to be forgiven. Under grace, you forgive because you have been forgiven. This is why it is called old covenant and new covenant. Knowing the difference is a game changer.

When it comes to forgiving others, there is a huge difference in what is required of us by the law, which is the old covenant, and grace, which is the new covenant. Under the old covenant, we forgive in order to be forgiven. The law requires us to do what God says, and when we do, He responds accordingly. Under grace (which is the new covenant), God did what He required from us and then gives us the freedom to respond to Him. The law tells us what we must do, and grace tells us what we get to do.

What makes forgiving and forgetting so confusing is we do not know when the law ended and grace began. When we turn the page from Malachi in the Old Testament and read Matthew, in the New Testament, we assume we are reading the New Covenant. Just because we are reading the New Testament does not mean we are reading the New Covenant.

According to the book of Hebrews, a covenant does not go into effect until the one who wrote it dies (Hebrews 9:11–22). The New Covenant of Grace did not begin until Jesus died on the cross. If this is too stretchy for you, I would encourage you to spend some time in the book of Galatians. "But when the fullness of the time had come, God sent forth His Son, born of a woman, *born under the law*" (Galatians 4:4 NKJV, emphasis added). What covenant was humankind under when Jesus was born? The law. When we use the law to define how God interacts with His people, truth gets blurred.

Let me give you a couple of illustrations to show you what I mean. The following has to do with forgiving and forgetting.

"And whenever you stand praying, if you have anything against anyone, forgive him that your Father in heaven may also forgive you your trespasses. But *if you do not forgive, neither will your Father in heaven forgive your trespasses*" (Mark 11:25–26 NKJV, emphasis added). I guess there is no need to say anything else about forgiving and forgetting. It is as clear as the nose on your face that in order for God to forgive us, it will require us to forgive others. That's what this verse says, and it is written in red.

Here are the words of Jesus found in Matthew's gospel: "For if you forgive men their trespasses, your heavenly Father will also forgive you. But if you do not forgive men their trespasses, neither will your Father forgive your trespasses" (Matthew 6:14–15 NKJV).

These passages leave us with no doubt that in order for us to be forgiven, we must forgive.

This is not a book on hermeneutics, but I do want to give some insight that will help you immensely in your personal Bible study. To keep things within context when you study scripture, ask yourself three questions: Who is speaking? To whom is he speaking? And when was he speaking?

Let's pose those three questions to these two passages on forgiving. There is no doubt as to who was speaking; it was Jesus. To whom was He speaking? His audience was His disciples who had gathered with Him on the mountainside. But most importantly, when did Jesus speak these words? Keep Galatians 4:4 in mind when you answer that question. Jesus was born under the law. When Jesus came to this earth, the only way a person could be in right standing with God was by keeping the law. God interacted with humanity based on their obedience to the law.

As children of God, we are now under a new covenant. This New Covenant was not inaugurated until Jesus died (Hebrews

9:15–22). God now interacts with people by grace. Grace is unmerited favor and is based on what God did for us. We are in right standing with God because we responded in faith to what He did to redeem us from our sins. He sent His son Jesus to shed His blood and to die on the cross in our place, so we who had no hope can now live with great expectancy.

Many Christians are living defeated lives because someone has thrown in their face Old Testament requirements for being forgiven: "The Bible says you have to forgive if you want to be forgiven." That is what the Bible says, but it was said before Jesus died. His death changed everything. Under grace, we forgive because we have been forgiven.

"Let all bitterness, wrath, anger, clamor, and evil speaking be put away from you, with all malice. And be kind to one another, tenderhearted, *forgiving one another, even as God in Christ forgave you*" (Ephesians 4:31–32 NKJV). Not only did my sweet soulmate embrace grace, she was an extender of grace to others, even those who hurt her by their actions or words. She forgave easily because she knew she had been forgiven. Once she forgave, she would never mention it again.

## Sabotaged Marriages

Far too many couples have wounded one another with their actions or words. They have sabotaged their own marriages. During heated moments, one or both may get *historical*. I bet I can guess what you are thinking: *You mean hysterical.* No, I meant to say historical. Unless we have forgiven and forgotten, we have the propensity to dredge up past events during emotional flareups, especially those that inflicted pain on us. That's being historical. A spouse may say she has forgiven, but the problem is she has never forgotten what was done. It is obvious she hasn't because she keeps bringing up her covenant partner's past transgressions. Knowing it or not, that is a festering sore that will never become a scar. It will remain a wound forever.

I'm certainly not inferring that forgiving and forgetting is easy to do. It is not. It may be one of the hardest things a person can ever do. But it is possible because God's Word says it is. And He would not tell us to do something if it were impossible to do.

Betty Ann was always the first to say, "I'm sorry," even when it was not her fault. And most of the time she had absolutely nothing to be sorry about. When we first got married, I was amazed how quickly she would say she was sorry. I'm thinking, *For what?* In her previous marriage, she had been lacerated by cutting words. She did not want anyone to feel that kind of pain, especially me.

Because of Betty Ann's weakened physical condition, the only place she felt comfortable and safe was on one of our couches. At this juncture in her fight with cancer, the last thing she needed was a fall.

One day I was sitting on the smaller couch next to her. We were engaged in small talk when I saw something move in the corner of my eye. The first thought I had was it was a piece of paper moved by the fan that was blowing on Betty Ann. But as soon I dismissed it, I saw it again.

This time I stood up to see what it was. It was a snake! In the house. I yelled, "Snake!"

In her weakened condition, Betty Ann launched off the couch like a rocket. I pulled the couch out and turned it over so I could see where this intruder had hidden. When I located it, I pinned its head with a broom so I could grab it behind its head. Once I had it secured in my hands, I took it outside and did what I needed to do. It was not venomous, but to me every snake is a king cobra. All snakes may not hurt you, but they will make you hurt yourself.

We had no idea how the snake got inside the house. Betty Ann guessed it came inside when I went to feed the dog. She was probably right because I did leave the door ajar when I went outside. That will be forever etched in my mind. A snake in the house.

This is exactly what has happened to a lot of marriages. The devil (snake) has slithered his way into our homes to wreak havoc. He is committed to the destruction of all marriages. Satan's job description is found in John 10:10, "The thief [snake] does not come except *to steal*, and *to kill*, and *to destroy*" (NKJV, emphasis added).

Since Genesis 2, Satan has been quite successful in carrying out his search-and-destroy mission. But there are limits to what he is able to accomplish. He can only do what we allow him to do. And for us to be ignorant of his game plan is to set ourselves up for an attack (2 Corinthians 2:1). Two of the biggest and deadliest weapons he has in his arsenal are unforgiveness, and unwillingness to forget. He is easily disarmed when we forgive and forget one another as quickly as possible.

## Forgiveness Is a Choice

To better understand what forgiveness is, it would be good to know what forgiveness is not. It is not about restoring a broken relationship. Some relationships need to remain severed because they are so toxic. So don't be confused if people you have forgiven are not back in your inner circle.

Forgiveness does not mean you surrender your emotional health and physical well-being to the person or persons who have abused you. Some people need to be removed from your life. Don't allow guilt to keep you vulnerable to being mistreated.

Forgiveness does not mean you can't establish perimeters. There are some areas in your life that you need to protect and place safeguards around. You can even put up a sign that says "Violators will be prosecuted." Prosecute to the fullest degree anyone who violates that order.

Forgiveness is more about you than anything else. Your mental and spiritual health are more important than the one you need to forgive. Choosing to forgive keeps you healthy and free. It keeps you from becoming a victim. Few people understand this. If we ever get ensnared by hurt, anger, and vindictiveness, it will not be long until bitterness has a firm grip on the control panels of our lives. Let me put it in Texas Panhandle vernacular: Forgiving and forgetting are the keys that keep the doors of hurt locked and the doors of free-living wide open.

Boiled down to its core? Forgiveness is a choice.

Betty Ann not only understood what forgiveness is, she lived it. My Proverbs Thirty-Two woman was quick to forgive, and she chose to forget. Forgetting is not having something removed from our memory. Some things can't be erased no matter how much time has elapsed since the injustice. It is choosing not to keep bringing it up.

Betty Ann never dwelt on the hurts from her past. That always impressed me, because I knew most of the things that had happened to her. If anyone had the right to hold on to a grudge, it was that lady. She had been through a lot, but she refused to allow the past to emotionally imprison her.

If we choose not to forgive, and we can, we will end up being controlled by the people who have violated our trust. Instead of us holding them captive, our resentments will keep us in bondage. Knowingly or unknowingly, we hand the control of our lives over to the people we refuse to forgive.

"To forgive is to set a prisoner free and discover that the prisoner was you"—Lewis B. Smedes, *Forgive and Forget: Healing the Hurts We Don't Deserve*

# 9

## She Loved the Unloved

MY PROVERBS THIRTY-TWO WOMAN HAD A STRONG AFFINITY for ladies who were victims of abuse, whether psychological or physical. It was easy for her to recognize someone who was being bullied. That was her experience for many years. She knew what it felt like to have no confidence in your own worth and self-respect. My sweet Betty Ann felt their pain; she knew how low self-esteem can keep a person from ever being who God created them to be and to have no hope for things to be different. She found it easy to love the unloved.

Before I continue, let me give you my first impression of Betty Ann before I really knew her. I saw her on Sundays, and I knew her name, but I did not know her. Every time we greeted one another, she had a forlorn look on her face. I seldom saw her smile. Come to think of it, I never saw her smile. I chalked it up as being her personality. These sarcastic thoughts went through my mind: "I'll bet she's a lot of fun to be around—not." I did not know her story, and I judged her too quickly, as did a lot of people. I know her story now, and it embarrasses me for having these thoughts.

There were seasons when she would lose a lot of weight. I remember one short span of time when she was nothing more than skin and bones. It had gotten everyone's attention. Again, I did not know what she was dealing with from her past, what she was going through in her present, or the hopelessness she had for a future that had anything good to offer. Life can be tough when you feel you are at the end of your rope and believe no one understands or cares. My Proverbs Thirty-Two woman knew firsthand what it feels like to think no one cares about you and believe you are unlovable. Now that I know her story, I am amazed she mustered enough spunk to keep going. I am so glad she did not throw in the towel like so many people do, because I would not be the man I am today if she had given up. She was one incredible lady. All she needed was for someone to love her unconditionally and give her the opportunity to love him back.

## You Don't Have to Smell like What You Have Gone Through

There is an incredible story in the book of Daniel about three young men, Shadrach, Meshach, and Abednego, who refused to bow and give their allegiance to an ungodly king. Their refusal to submit to this decree was going to get them tossed into a fiery furnace. In spite of this threat, they would not capitulate to the orders given to them by King Nebuchadnezzar. The king followed through with his threat—all three men were cast into a fiery furnace. Because they refused to bow, they did not burn.

"And the satraps, administrators, governors, and the king's counselors gathered together, and they saw these men on whose bodies *the fire had no power*, the hair of their head was not singed nor were their garments affected, *and the smell of fire was not on them*" (Daniel 3:27 NKJV, emphasis added).

Look at this: When these three young men came out of the furnace, they did not smell like smoke. Their hair and clothes were not singed. The only thing that burned was the cords that had them bound. They did not smell like what they had been through.

This describes Betty Ann to the nth degree. Even in her deepest pain she would not surrender or give her allegiance to it, even though there were times she found herself on the threshold of waving the white flag of surrender. But she kept going when her *want-to* was running on empty. She refused to bow and did not burn. Not only that, she did not smell like what she had been through. That cannot be said about most of us.

One day, she and I were talking about our childhood days, how we were raised, and some of the experiences we had in our growing-up years. In this conversation she told me her mother never once told her she was pretty, smart, or even said, "I love you." Yet Betty Ann never held that against her. She loved her mother.

Just before my sweet covenant partner left this physical realm to be with her Lord and Savior, Jesus Christ, we were having a talk about Jesus, heaven, and what it must be like to be in His forever presence.

I asked Betty Ann, "Do you think about Jesus very much?"

Her response was, "All the time." And then, without hesitating, she said, "I think about my mother all the time too. I'm looking forward to seeing her again."

My Proverbs Thirty-Two woman did not smell like the rejection she had been through. She was so quick to forgive and let go of those who spitefully used and abused her.

Betty Ann had a sixth sense that went on alert when she was around a lady who was going through what Betty Ann had been through. Because she allowed God to heal her of all the pain and abuse she had gone through, her emotional wounds had become scars. That is what a scar is, a healed wound. She used those scars as her testimony to help hurting women stay on their feet. Her place of business was more than a lady's boutique, it was her pulpit, her mission field. She never missed an opportunity to minister to a hurting soul.

Over the last fifty years, I have ministered to many people who carry the smell of their hurtful events. I remember visiting a person once who was in emotional turmoil over his divorce. His feelings were raw and sensitive. At times he lost it emotionally and cried uncontrollably. Because he was in such pain, I assumed his divorce was in progress or had taken place recently. I was taken aback when he told me it had been finalized seventeen years ago. Seventeen years is a long time to smell like what you have been through.

During Betty Ann's high school years, she was the target of a lot of bullying. On one occasion her so-called-friends came up with a scheme to embarrass her. They told her it would be cool if everyone brought their favorite baby dolls to school. Of course, they were not going to follow through with it themselves. What would their classmates say about their immaturity? High school girls don't play with dolls.

The day was set for this event to happen, and guess who was the only one to bring their doll to school. It makes me tear up just sharing this story. I will never forget the day Betty Ann told me about what those girls did to her. My emotions went off the charts. She told me how humiliating that moment was for her. This kind of emotional bullying can do irreparable damage to one's psychological health. Bullying in any shape or form can have immediate long-term effects on those involved, and that includes those who have witnessed the bullying. To bully someone is to make that victim feel less about who she is as a person.

For twenty years Betty Ann was in a marriage that was filled with unfaithfulness, extreme verbal abuse, and seasons of physical violence. Not many people knew the extent of the horrific treatment she experienced. I always enjoyed watching the faces of the people who listened to her testimony, especially those who knew her pretty well. They were stunned.

It was not uncommon to hear someone say, "How in the world can you be so sweet and trusting considering what you have experienced?" or "As long as I've known you, I had no idea what you have been through," and "I never would have guessed it, because your smile is infectious and your demeanor is so sweet."

That was my J.21 covenant partner. She did not hold grudges or contempt for anyone, including those who were unkind or had spitefully used her. Betty Ann did not smell like what she had been through. This was a choice she made out of her own free will. She was one of the kindest, most forgiving people I have ever known in my life.

Betty Ann came to know, in a personal way, how God can heal emotional wounds. With God's healing she was able to minister to many ladies who had been wounded too. She understood how they felt, and she had empathy for those who had lost hope of things ever being better. Her scars became her greatest assets in binding the wounds of those who had been bullied.

### Betty Ann Was Always for the Underdog

Betty Ann could always be found in the corner of those who felt they had little to no chance at winning in this thing called life. She knew what life was like in that corner, because she had been there by herself many times, with no one to help or fight with her. She had an affinity for the underdog, and they knew it.

This is why she was so quick to help the ladies who came into her boutique, especially those who she discerned needed more than clothes. They needed spiritual healing. Fashions are constantly changing, but a wounded spirit can incarcerate a soul for a lifetime. Betty Ann could recognize an orphan spirit in a heartbeat. She didn't just make sure these ladies got the clothes they needed, she loved on them with hugs and the comfort that came out of the crucible of her own experiences. She was an underdog's biggest fan.

When we sold our building and business, I had an eye-opening discovery. Betty Ann was fighting for her earthly life with cancer, so she could not help with removing our personal belongings from the boutique. As I was cleaning out some of the file cabinets, I came across a file folder I had never seen before. It was filled with invoices for clothes she had gifted needy ladies with. Their names were omitted from the receipts because she wanted to protect their identities. She did not want any embarrassment to come to these ladies by making this information known. That is my J.21 covenant partner.

If I were to tell you how much the clothes cost that she gifted to ladies in need each year, you probably would not believe it, so I will keep it to myself. This was not a one-time thing. I found a receipt for every year she had her boutique. I will say that the amount would blow your mind. It did mine, and I know the girl. Betty Ann never forgot how it felt not to have things you need, much less want. She was always for the underdog.

At Betty Ann's home-going celebration service, I heard testimony after testimony from ladies she had blessed. Women who had no hope for tomorrow until they met my sweet wife. She had made sure their needs were met. Many stated they wouldn't be on their feet today without her. She was Jesus to them wrapped in human skin. How good is that? Betty Ann championed the underdog.

## Betty Ann Would Never Write a Person Off

We do not find it difficult to love people who reciprocate their love in a corresponding way. But don't ask us to love people who have neglected us or not been there when we desperately needed them, especially if they are family. Families need to be close to one another, and should be, but sometimes that is not in the cards we have been dealt. We cannot make people love. That is actually a good thing. What kind of love would it be if we had the power to make people love us? It would be unnatural and mechanical.

The Word of God says, "We love each other because he loved us first" (1 John 4:19 NLT). When we grasp the love that God has for us, we will find it much easier to love those who are hard to love. My Proverbs Thirty-Two woman never lost her awe of how much she was loved by God, which made it easier for her to love the unlovable. If we never come to realize God's affection for us, we will not be able to demonstrate our love to others, especially family. We can talk about God's love, but if we refuse to love those who need to be loved, we do not grasp the love of God.

I hear people say all the time, "I can't and won't forgive them. They don't deserve my forgiveness." I understand, but let's flip the coin over. Did we deserve God's love? Were we so good that God could not help but love us? If you say yes, I encourage you to find yourself a Proverbs Thirty-Two woman or man and have her or him minister to you. You need help whether you know it or not.

"Wayne, I've been praying about something. I think I'm going to visit my dad to see if we can reconcile our differences. When I was small, we had a great daddy-daughter relationship. He would take me to church, and that became a special time for me. What do you think?"

I knew this lady very well. She would not seek to do anything that she had not prayed through. I gave her my blessings. I knew it had to be a difficult decision for her, because she and her dad had not seen each other but once or twice in several years. They had talked to each other on the phone, but not on a regular basis.

There was a lady in our church family who was a good friend to my wife. She had gone shopping with Betty Ann many times to serve as a model for the new clothing styles that constantly came out. This made it easier for Betty Ann to see what the outfits would look like with someone wearing them. They would usually spend two to three days at market. She asked her friend if she would go with her to see her dad. He was living in a neighboring state, and she would feel more comfortable with a traveling partner. Her friend said she would be more than happy to go with her.

They spent two days with Betty Ann's dad. During this short period, their relationship was restored. From that moment on, Betty Ann and her dad talked by phone almost every day. Few days passed without him calling to check on her, and vice versa.

Three weeks after Betty Ann left to be with Jesus, her dad called her personal cell phone. He was getting up in age and is battling dementia, so I'm sure he had a momentary loss of reality. It was a sobering moment for me as well. I did not answer the phone because I did not want to embarrass him or cause any emotional trauma. His call to check on his girl confirmed in my spirit that the reconciliation between him and his oldest daughter was legit.

Oftentimes we want from others what we are not willing to give them—forgiveness. Betty Ann was quick to forgive and release people. She embraced the words Paul used when he wrote his letter to the Christians who lived in Rome. *"If it is possible, as much as it depends on you,* live peaceably with all men" (Romans 12:18 NKJV, emphasis added). If it is possible. It may not be. Another translation renders it this way: "Do all that you can to live in peace with everyone" (Romans 12:18 NLT). We don't need to apply any hermeneutical principles to this verse, do we? It speaks for itself and does not need any help from us to interpret its meaning.

## Betty Ann Had an Empathetic Spirit

It was natural for Betty Ann to feel empathy for hurting people, especially women. She knew firsthand how rejection can destroy a person's self-esteem. She knew the pain verbal abuse can inflict on someone. She understood the lonely depression of not having someone you can trust help you get out of the emotional pit you had been shoved into. She could spot victims of physical abuse a mile away. She felt their pain. She was able to vicariously experience the feelings of the hurting: Nothing short of amazing.

It was easy for her to feel and understand the pain others found themselves in. She had been there, and God had miraculously healed her from all her wounds. She was a good steward of her healing, using it to help heal others.

## She Guarded Her Speech

My wife's ability to guard what came out of her mouth always fascinated me. I was just the opposite. Sometimes my greatest accomplishment was keeping my mouth closed. I was like Simon Peter for most of my life. I only opened my mouth to insert another foot. Being with her and observing how she conducted her life affected me in a good way.

So much so that it caught the attention of my son. He asked me one day, "Dad, what's happened to you? You're not the same man I've known all my life. You're at such peace."

Today, I find it much easier to guard my mouth and watch my words because of the influence Betty Ann had on me.

One day we had an unpleasant encounter with someone Betty Ann and I both love. He was saying things that were not true, and I wanted him to know how I felt, so I gave him a piece of my mind, even though I knew I needed it all. Betty Ann never said a word. She stayed in peace.

On our way home, I was still venting about what had happened. I asked her why she didn't say anything.

She said, "Cowboy, you will always remain in control of your words as long as you don't speak them. Once you release them, you can never take them back or repair the damage they may cause." To this day I have no clue what she meant. Yeah, right. Don't judge me. To paraphrase Abe Lincoln: People may think you are a fool, so why open your mouth and remove all doubt?

All the time we dated, and during our entire marriage, she never used cutting words to hurt me or put me in my place. She was always uplifting and encouraging. I use to tell her all the time when she was bragging on me, "I love it when you lie, sweetheart."

She would say, "I don't lie, Cowboy." Her words were always positive and seasoned with experience. She had not forgotten how much hurt can be inflicted on a person by the use of words. She was not going to do unto others what was done to her.

Those who are hurting need a safe zone. They need a person who is quick to hear and slow to speak (James 1:19). Maybe that's why God gave us two ears and one mouth. We need to do twice as much listening than speaking.

Sometimes people who are hurting just needs someone to listen to them vent their pain. This is why Betty Ann was able to help so many women. She knew firsthand what it is like not to have an outlet where she could express her feelings of complete hopelessness without being judged, or becoming a victim of gossip. Oftentimes people will find a great measure of healing simply by having the freedom to unload the baggage they are carrying inside them.

My precious wife had not forgotten what it was like to feel that you are totally alone, with no hope of a better tomorrow. Hurting women were drawn to her like moths to a flame. She provided them with a safe place and the confidentiality they needed so desperately. And they seized it.

If ladies asked her not to divulge what they had told her, she honored their request. She did not tell me what someone told her if she had asked Betty Ann to keep it between them. I loved that about my once-in-a-lifetime marriage covenant partner. There were many occasions when we would be talking to a lady who had been ministered to by Betty Ann. During our three-way conversation, the individual we were talking to would talk about what she had told Betty Ann in confidence. It did not take long for her to see the blank look on my face.

She would say to my wife, "You didn't tell Wayne what we talked about?" It was assumed she had since we were husband and wife.

When she told them no, she had not, because she had asked Betty Ann not to tell anyone what they had talked about, she was floored. She could be trusted; she would keep a confidence. This is why the people who knew her said she was legit, and she was.

## She Was a Wife of Noble Character

"Who can find a virtuous and capable wife? She is more precious than rubies. Her husband can trust her, and she will greatly enrich his life. She brings him good, not harm, all the days of her life" (Proverbs 31:10–12 NLT).

"Her children stand and bless her. Her husband praises her: There are many virtuous and capable women in the world, but you surpass them all! Charm is deceitful, and beauty does not last, but a woman who fears the Lord will be greatly praised. Reward her for all she has done. Let her deeds publicly declare her praise" (Proverbs 31:28–31 NLT).

My Proverbs Thirty-Two woman always had a sweet smile on her face, a giggle in her voice, and a soft, warm spirit. People who knew her for years agree. She had a very special place in her heart for the unloved. She gave to them what the Lord had given to her: Unconditional love. This is a rare person.

But she could be a prankster. I could write a chapter on that, but I'm not sure the statute of limitations has run out on most of her (our) shenanigans. At times she was willing to be my partner in crime. We made a good team, too.

# 10

## *She Loved Her Jesus*

THERE WAS NEVER A DOUBT WHERE MY SWEET WIFE STOOD when it came to loving her Jesus. She made no bones about it. Her relationship with Christ was not a Sunday affair. Jesus was her life, and she was not ashamed or intimidated to let people know it. You never had to wonder where Betty Ann stood when it came to being a person of faith. She was not perfect by any stretch of the imagination, but she knew she was loved by a perfect God.

### *She Did Not Hide Her Faith*

The community of faith is filled with too many secret saints. They appear on Sunday mornings and then disappear during the week. Fear of being ridiculed for their faith, these folks find comfort and safety by staying in the shadows. I call them God's secret agents. This was not so with my precious Betty Ann. People who knew her will tell you she would witness at the drop of a hat. And she would drop the hat if she had to. She had no problem praying for someone in public or sharing her testimony. She had a sensitivity to the prompting of the Spirit to minister to anyone, anywhere, at any time. I never knew my Proverbs Thirty-Two woman to hide her faith. When it came to expressing her love for Christ, she was not a spectator. She was a participator.

My covenant partner knew something about God's grace that most Christians never come to know. If grace cannot change the way you live your life, then grace cannot save your soul, either. She knew she had been a recipient of God's amazing grace and she did not find it difficult to extend that same amazing grace to others. She loved her Jesus!

She and I were sitting with our small group under a pavilion taking communion at the Garden Tomb in Israel. It was one of those sweet moments that most people dream about having but never experience. There was a holy hush present as we sat there reflecting on how good our heavenly Father is to us, even with all our faults and failures. Several pavilions in the Garden Tomb area were filled with people from all over the world. Unexpectedly, light raindrops began to splatter on top of the covering where we were sitting. It did not disturb the peace that was present. If anything, it was enhanced.

During this quiet moment, as the drops of rain fell, my dear wife began singing a song that C. Austin Miles wrote in 1913, called "In the Garden":

> I come to the garden alone,
> While the dew is still on the roses,
> And the voice I hear, falling on my ear,
> The Son of God discloses.
>
> And He walks with me, and He talks with me,
> And He tells me I am His own,

And the joy we share as we tarry there
None other has ever known.

He speaks and the sound of His voice
Is so sweet, the birds hush their singing,
And the melody that He gave to me
Within my heart is ringing.

And He walks with me, and He talks with me,
And He tells me I am His own,
And the joy we share as we tarry there,
None other has ever known.

I'd stay in the garden with Him
Tho' the night around me be falling,
But He bids me go, thro' the voice of woe,
His voice to me is calling.

And He walks with me, and He talks with me,
And He tells me I am His own,
And the joy we share as we tarry there,
None other has ever known.

I can still hear my beloved's voice in my innermost being as if this special moment had happened yesterday.

Even though there were many languages present that day, everyone recognized the song she was singing. Without any prompting, the people under the other pavilions began to sing along with us: Everyone in their native tongue. The whole garden was filled with praise and adoration to the King of kings, and the Lord of lords. This incredible experience was not in the difference of languages that had joined together in unison to sing this song, it was the connecting of hearts of everyone present at the Garden Tomb. For one specific moment, everyone's focus was on Jesus. The only way I can describe it is like this: it was a moment when heaven kissed earth. Once again, my beautiful covenant partner did not hide her faith.

## *She Talked to God As If He Were Sitting Next to Her*

I mentioned in chapter 1 that Betty Ann was an active member of the prayer ministry at the church I pastored. It was a small intercessory prayer group but a powerful one. During our prayer time each person had a designated moment when they would pray out loud. Everyone on the prayer team loved it when it came time for Betty Ann to pray. Occasionally we would peek to see if Jesus was sitting next to her. The conversation she was having with Him was so personal, warm, and intimate. She talked to Him the way all children should talk to their heavenly Father. Prayer for her was not a monologue, it was a dialogue. She talked to the Lord as you would talk to a special friend.

What Betty Ann did in that prayer ministry time, she did in our home as my covenant partner. We often took communion together and prayed. When she prayed, she did not just touch the hem of Jesus's garment like the woman did in Mark 5:27–28, she crawled up in his lap. As we would say in the Texas Panhandle, she loved her some Jesus.

Anytime we considered buying something major or making an investment, that particular thing became our prayer focus. We would seek the Lord's wisdom and direction. Both of us had made some poor choices in our pasts, and we did not want to repeat them. Once something became our prayer focus, she would find something tangible that represented what we were seeking the Lord's wisdom for. She would use whatever that may have been to represent what we were believing God for.

Let me give you an example. We spotted some land we wanted to buy to build our future home on. This was prime land, and we knew it would not be on the market for long. A quick decision had to be made, but we did not want to make a mistake, because this purchase would cost a considerable amount of money. We walked this piece of property many times as we prayed for Holy Spirit's guidance. It was a ten-acre tract, so each prayer session took some time. I noticed Betty Ann was picking up handfuls of dirt as she walked and prayed. I never asked her what she was doing or why.

One day as I was walking past a table in our den, I noticed a ceramic container I had never seen before. On one side were these words: "With God all things are possible." This was a quote from Matthew 19:26. I was curious, so I opened the lid. Inside was some of the dirt she had picked up during our prayer walks. I'll bet you can guess what happened. Yes, we bought the land. And it turned out to be one incredible investment. This was not an isolated event. It was Betty Ann's lifestyle. She lived her faith and was unabashed about it.

## She Had a Quiet Spirit

Betty Ann's love for Jesus, and knowing He loved her, kept her calm and still no matter what was going on around her. Times of chaos did not move her out of peace. She was able to restrain her speech and emotions when others were going berserk. The following describes Betty Ann to a tee: "Do not let adornment be merely outward—arranging the hair, wearing gold, or putting on fine apparel—rather let it be *the hidden person of the heart*, with the incorruptible beauty of *a gentle and quiet spirit* which is very precious in the sight of God" (1 Peter 3:3–4 NKJV, emphasis added).

The peace of God appropriated is the key to having a quiet spirit. It is a choice we all have to make. Did you notice I said it is a choice? You may be thinking, *Not me. I'm a 220-volt wired into a 110-volt outlet. It is impossible for me to not spark and short out when there is a spirit of panic surrounding me.* I think we should remove the word *can't* from our conversation. It is a matter of *want to.* How desperate are we to be held in the arms of quiet peace?

In all the years we were married, I never once saw her lose her peace. This in no way means there were not times when she was concerned about something. But she never lost sight that Christ was her life; therefore, He was her peace (Ephesians 2:14). Watching how she reacted and responded to challenges impacted my life. I saw in her what I desperately wanted. I am a man of peace today because I was blessed to be in covenant with a lady who lived her life in peace. She fleshed out what every human being is looking for—a life of tranquility. Her state of calmness came from knowing her new creation identity in Christ. Her spirit of peace and quietness radically transformed the environment in our home. I cannot tell you how many times a visitor will say, "You can feel the peace that is in your home." You really can.

Several years ago, my son and his beautiful family came to spend some time with us. While we were sitting on the back patio engaged in small talk, he said, "Dad, there's something different about you. What is it?"

My son knows his dad well. He has seen me in my best moments and my worst. Actually, his question caught me off guard. I had no idea why he would ask such a question. I do recall how I responded: "I don't know what you're talking about, son." I really didn't.

He said, "I've never seen you at such peace. What's happened to you?"

His question opened the door for me to share how the revelation of the exchanged life had set me free. It also gave me the opportunity to brag on Betty Ann and how God used her to give me the life I had always dreamed of having but did not believe it would ever happen.

To this day, you can feel the presence of God's peace in our home, even though my Proverbs Thirty-Two woman is now at home with her Jesus. What she left is still living on—a quiet spirit that can still be felt.

## She Was Our Resident Theologian

I tell people all the time that I may be the seminary graduate in our home, but Betty Ann is the resident theologian. You can have a seminary degree and still be a mile wide and an inch deep. When it came to the things of God, my covenant partner was deep and wide.

It is impossible for me to count the number of times I would be waxing eloquent about some systematic theological or doctrinal point, and all she would do was look at me with her warm smile and loving eyes. She never interrupted me during my presentation.

When I concluded with my apologetics, she would say something like, "God is so good, isn't He?" as she nodded affirmingly.

I can espouse systematic theology in a way that makes me look like I am in the know. It comes out of my head. Betty Ann fleshed out theological soundness from her heart.

Her influence on me has caused me to shift gears. I am still a proponent for sound doctrine, but I've learned (from her) that there is a greater knowledge. It is found in the lyrics of the song "Jesus Loves Me, This I Know" by Anna Bartlett Warner, written in 1859.

Jesus loves me! This I know,
For the Bible tells me so;
Little ones to Him belong,
They are weak, but He is strong.
Refrain:
Yes, Jesus loves me!
Yes, Jesus loves me!
Yes, Jesus loves me!
The Bible tells me so.

These lyrics are all we need in order to have a love affair with Jesus. Very few people ever discover how much Jesus loves them, even though the Bible tells them so. If or when they do, they cannot help but love Him in return. This was more than a sweet little song that you sing to children for Betty Ann. These words were her testimony. She kept things profoundly simple, which made them simply profound.

## She Was God's Special Gift to Me

"I have never seen two people love each other the way you guys do." These words were spoken often by people who hung around us for any period of time. No one ever heard us belittle the other one in public, even in gest. It never happened because we never did that privately either. This sweet lady always built me up with her words and actions. This created within me the desire to be the kind of person she said I was. As Proverbs 31 says, when a man finds a good woman, he finds a treasure. I won the lottery.

Of all the scriptures I could choose to define our marriage, this one stands out above them all: *"The heart of her husband safely trusts her,* so he will have no lack of grain. She does him good and not evil *all the days of her life"* (Proverbs 31:11–12 NKJV, emphasis added). His heart trusts her! There was never a moment when I did not trust B. A. She never had a concern about trusting me. This made our marriage even stronger. She wanted to be with me, and I wanted to be with her. Neither one of us ever doubted that. We were blessed to have the very thing we thought we would never have—a soulmate who wanted to be with you.

In most of my preaching engagements, Betty Ann was right by my side, and it was because she wanted to be. Wherever we were going, I would tell her how thankful and blessed I was to have her along side of me.

She would say something like, "I'm with you, Cowboy, because I want to be with you." And she did, and I knew it. There were many times we did not get home until the wee hours of the morning, but never once did she complain.

When God began to open doors for me to go out of the country to minister, Betty Ann was unable to go, with the exception of Israel. She had a boutique to oversee, and we had a young child at home. But no matter what time of day or night I returned, she and Alex would be standing at the front door to welcome me. They would greet me with a big hug and kiss. Home felt so good! When your covenant partner wants to be with you, loves you, and trusts you, going home is always a pleasant experience. I always looked forward to seeing my beloved. I wanted to be with the one that I was in covenant with.

After Betty Ann went to be with Jesus, there came a time when I felt like I needed to clean out a couple of closets and rearrange a few things. In the process, I found notebook after notebook of sermon notes of mine penned by her own hand. I was amazed. Her notes were better than the messages I had preached. Once again, it was confirmed, not only did she want to be with me, she went to participate in what God was doing, not to be a spectator.

"Good job, Cowboy, good job," was usually what she said after I delivered my message.

## She Was My Confidant

There was nothing that I could not talk to Betty Ann about. She never judged me for my shortcomings or belittled me if I made a bad business decision. Most men do not mind talking about their successes but are reluctant when it comes to sharing their defeats. She was my confidant. Betty Ann was my safe place. We both were open books for the other one to read. There were no secrets between us, because we knew the other one was always in our corner no matter what. Our love for each other was unconditional. We gave each other room to make mistakes and not be judged. This is so freeing. Neither one of us had ever been in a relationship like this.

There is a passage in the book of Jeremiah that encapsulates Betty Ann's ability to love me unconditionally.

> Blessed [happy] is the man *who trusts in the Lord*, and *whose hope* [confidence] *is in the Lord*. For he shall be like a tree planted [stable] by the waters, which spreads out its roots by the river, and *will not fear* when heat comes, but its leaf will be green, and *will not be anxious* in the year of drought, nor will cease from yielding fruit. (Jeremiah 17:7–8 NKJV, emphasis added)

These verses epitomize my Betty Ann's life. She found her hope and confidence in the Lord, and because of that, unsettling moments never unmoored her from her faith in Jesus. She always stayed anchored no matter how intense the storms had been. Her confidence and faith in the Lord kept her from coming unraveled when others were coming apart at the seams.

## God Gave Betty Ann the Desires of Her Heart

Betty Ann knew that her problems did not move God; the content of her heart did. She had in Jesus what she knew could not be taken away. My beloved Proverbs Thirty-Two woman was emotionally and spiritually stable. She understood that Jesus was the anchor of her soul, so she placed her trust in Him. "*Trust* in the Lord with all your heart; do not depend on your own understanding. *Seek* his will in all you do, and he will show you which path to take" (Proverbs 3:5–6 NLT, emphasis added).

In the thirty-seventh chapter of the book of Psalms, David gives us the formula for living a quiet and peaceful life: Trust, delight, Commit. Betty Ann not only could recite this verse from her heart, she lived it.

"*Trust* in the Lord, and do good; dwell in the land, and feed on His faithfulness" (Psalm 37:3 NKJV, emphasis added).

"*Delight* yourself also in the Lord, and He shall give you the desires of your heart" (Psalm 37:4 NKJV; emphasis added).

"*Commit* your way to the Lord, trust also in Him, and He shall bring it to pass" (Psalm 37:5 NKJV, emphasis added).

# 11

## The Report No One Wants to Hear

I was about to leave for a three-day men's retreat in the beautiful mountains of New Mexico. Everything was packed and loaded in my truck. I was going through the house with my checklist to make sure I had not forgotten anything. That was when Betty Ann stopped me in the bathroom and said she wanted me to feel a hard lump in her left breast.

The spot was hard and alarmingly large. I asked her what she thought it might be. The look on her face told me what she was thinking. I suggested she call her doctor immediately and set up an appointment, the sooner the better.

She made the call and was told she could not see the doctor until the following Monday. That worked out well for both of us because I would be home from the retreat early Sunday evening. I wanted to be with her when she had her appointment.

After a brief physical examination, the doctor told us his concern was the lump could be cancerous. He wanted to set up another appointment to have a biopsy done. It seemed like forever for that day to come, but it finally did. It was a pretty quiet ride from our home to the cancer center that was forty-five miles away. We both were in deep thought.

We had been in the waiting room for about thirty minutes when they called her name. I leaned over and gave her a kiss as she got up to follow the nurse to where they would do the biopsy. I told her that everything was going to be OK and that I loved her. She smiled and winked at me.

After what seemed like an eternity, a staff member of the cancer center who we personally know came walking up to me and told me Betty Ann needed to see me immediately. My heart flipped over as I got up to follow her. She did not say another word to me.

When I walked into the room, Betty Ann lost it emotionally. It did not take a rocket scientist to know the report was not a good one. The nurse in charge informed me what the doctor suspected about the lump. He told Betty Ann he was convinced the tissues he had removed for the pathologist to examine were cancerous.

It was a report no one wanted to hear.

## The Process Began

Our next meeting was with an oncologist and a radiologist. After another quick exam, they gave us the treatment protocol they would follow in treating the cancer that was attacking Betty Ann's body. They listed her medical condition as stage 3 cancer. Their plan was to give her five chemo treatments, wait four to five weeks, and then do a complete mastectomy and reconstructive surgery. After another six weeks she would receive five radiation treatments.

We gave our consent to follow the doctor's recommendations on treating the cancer they feared might be spreading rapidly.

Betty Ann and I had just about come to terms with the procedures the doctors had recommended when we got a phone call from the radiologist we were not expecting. The cancer had metastasized to her liver. They were concerned that it may have spread to other parts of her body as well.

The stage 3 cancer they had diagnosed her with was now elevated to stage 4. The treatment regimen they had prescribed was taken off the table. Another consultation with the oncologist was set up for us to discuss what treatments they recommended we pursue now. You can imagine the emotional rollercoaster we were on. It was very challenging to say the least.

We're back in the cancer treatment facility again. This time it was to meet with the oncologist to hear another report and to give us the opportunity to ask questions. Betty Ann and I, along with our youngest daughter, Alex, listened as the doctor told us what they found and suspected. We were told that the cancer could not be cured and that chemotherapy was our only option to extend Betty Ann's life. All three of us sat in stunned silence as they shared their findings. It was like having a bad dream. Surely we were going to wake up soon.

After the doctor finished giving us the diagnosis, I asked for a prognosis. I wanted to know how much time he thought we had.

I will never forget how my question was answered: Betty Ann had about five years to live. When the doctor said this, the room got deafeningly quiet. Reality had smacked us in the face. I looked at our daughter and she had a blank stare. She just heard that it was possible that she only had about five years to be with her mother.

Betty Ann sat quietly and never said a word. But you could tell she was processing the information they had just given us.

I remember the next thing I said without thinking: "The report that you just gave us will never come out of our mouths." And it did not. We never mentioned the prognosis that we were told to anyone, and we never talked about it at home. We chose not to make their prognosis report our testimony. Little did we know that was the day we began our six-and-a-half-year journey that would be life transforming. It would be the longest and most challenging season in our lives.

## The Six-and-a-Half-Year Journey

This time frame was filled with some highs and some extremely low lows. There were days when we soared with eagles, and other days it felt like we had been run over by a bus. Life for us had truly become a one-day-at-a-time venture.

In the early stages of her chemo treatments, she experienced a lot of pain. Her body was trying to adjust to all the chemo and meds being pumped into her body. Betty Ann was never one to complain, and when I say never, I mean never.

One day I sat beside her on the couch. She leaned into me, putting her head on my shoulder. In the midst of excruciating pain and tears she said, "Wayne, don't let me die. Please don't let me die."

There was absolutely nothing that I would not have done for my soulmate. Nothing. But she had just asked me to do something that was impossible for me to do. We sat there holding each other as we wept uncontrollably. My Proverbs Thirty-Two woman was engaged in a battle for her physical life. And we both knew it.

The hair on her head began to fall out just like they told us it would. Even though you have been told what to expect, sometimes you're not ready when it happens. During a visit by both of our daughters, Brooke and Alex, along with her sister, Marteal, Betty Ann asked the girls if they would shave what little hair she had left on her head. You can imagine how emotional that moment was. All I could do was hold her hand as the girls did what they were asked to do. Her sister stood quietly by my side as the girls shaved their mother's head. Reality was beginning to set in.

Over the next six-and-a-half years, Betty Ann had 109 chemo treatments and her liver was radiated twenty times. She never wobbled in her faith or trust in God. She kept a positive attitude through it all. Betty Ann was a legitimate Proverbs Thirty-Two woman. Have you noticed that people are like teabags? You really never know what's inside them until they are in hot water. What comes out is whatever is on the inside. During this hot-water season for Betty Ann, nothing ever came out of her but grace.

## Betty Ann's Physical Condition Worsens

During the last two and half years of Betty Ann's battle with cancer, we both knew our time together in this earthly realm was nearing an end. We never talked to anyone about what we were feeling, and it was never a conversation we had with one another. When you are truly one in covenant as soulmates, you know things without having to say them. No one knew me better than my beloved, and no one knew her better than I did. I'm convinced this is one of the reasons our marriage was filled with such peace, from the beginning all the way to the end.

I have a new respect and deep admiration for personal caregivers. The deeper we got into the last two years of Betty Ann's struggle with that insidious enemy called cancer, the more her need for personal care increased dramatically. Her everyday needs became my responsibility, and I am so thankful the Lord allowed me to have that honor and privilege. I had no doubt she would do the same for me if the roles were reversed.

She often said to me, "Thank you, darling, for being such a good helper." Even in her most miserable moments she was quick to tell me how appreciative she was for me taking care of her. That was my Proverbs Thirty-Two woman.

Betty Ann never wanted our girls to know how bad she was feeling. Extreme nausea began to attack her on a regular basis. This condition was caused by all the chemicals absorbed by her body and from all the meds she was taking. I could not begin to count the number of times she would violently disgorge the contents of her stomach: Cleanup was never a pleasant chore.

Oftentimes one of the girls would call when she was in the middle of one of those episodes, and ask, "How are you feeling, Mother?"

She would always say, "Fine." I'm down on the floor cleaning up vomit and she says, "I'm fine." She did not want to upset the girls by telling them how she was really feeling. But that was Betty Ann. She was always thinking about others.

It was a nine-hour drive to go see our girls. I did my best to make sure she got to spend as much time with them as possible, even though the trip would set her back for days.

One night while we were visiting the girls, she got up in the middle of the night to get a drink of water. I heard her when she got out of bed. I fell back to sleep. When I woke up, a couple of hours had passed and she was still not back in bed. I jumped up and went to check on her. I could not find her in the kitchen, the bathroom, or the living room. My heart raced. When I opened up our grandson's bedroom door, there she was, lying on the floor in a fetal position. She had covered herself with a bath towel. It was impossible for her to get up because she was so weak. I had to go get our son-in-law to help me get her back on her feet.

When I asked her why she didn't call out for help when she fell, she said, "I knew you would come looking for me."

That girl had complete trust in me. Again, she did not want to inconvenience anyone because of her needs. She would have laid there all night if that was what she had to do. She was not going to interrupt anyone's sleep if she could help it. Life for others was more important than the life she had.

Soon after that episode she went downhill fast. It got to where she could not get up off the couch without assistance. She had a difficult time just turning over. During the night I would see her reaching out, trying to get a grip on top of the couch in an attempt to get some leverage so she could change positions. It was gut-wrenching to watch. I always had a battle going on in my thought life: Do I help, or do I allow her to do this on her own?

One night we were both exhausted. Our day had been filled with physical challenges. Needless to say it did not take long for me to fall asleep. I normally cat napped during the night and was awake every time she needed something. That was definitely a God thing because I have always been a sound sleeper.

I never heard her get up. How she was able to get off the couch and into the mobile chair that we used to move her to where she needed to go is beyond me. All of a sudden I woke up and saw that she was not on the couch. When I looked down the hall, I saw her.

She was stuck in the middle of the hallway, slumped over and pawing at the floor with her left leg trying to get some traction so she could move herself to the bathroom. I jumped up and ran to help her. Why in the world did she do that? I will tell you why. She knew I was tired and desperately needed some rest. Instead of interrupting my sleep by waking me to help her to the bathroom, she put herself in jeopardy.

Her thoughts were always on me and what I needed. That was true for our entire marriage. She wanted me to get some sleep. That scene of her in the hallway flashes in my mind's eye all the time. And each time it does, I lose it emotionally. That was the epitome of the love she had for me. Hopefully by now you are beginning to see why I call her my Proverbs Thirty-Two woman. Her love and commitment to me were unconditional.

## She Had all the Chemo Her Body Could Handle

As I have already said, this incredible lady had 109 chemo treatments. I have never heard of anyone having that many, or close to it. The oncologist assured me that many people have had more than that. I tip my hat to those folks. Those people are true warriors.

It was time for her to have treatment number 110. It was obvious to me that she could not endure another treatment. She was not able to get off the couch, even with my assistance. Groggy, dazed, weak, and unsteady is the best way I could describe her. When I told her I did not feel she could or should have another chemo treatment, you could see the relief on her face. She was done; there would be no more treatments. The countdown of the days we had left together began. We both knew this day was coming and were prepared for it. Prepared, yes—but not ready.

Betty Ann was physically spent. She had fought the good fight, kept the faith, and was prepared to meet her Jesus. She also missed her mother and longed to see her again. I have already shared this moment in a previous chapter, but I want to repeat it. I know she was ready for her departure because one day I asked her if she thought about Jesus much. I knew she did. I just wanted to see if I could initiate a conversation about her impending earthly departure.

She responded, "Yes, I do. I think about Jesus all the time. I also think about my mother, and I miss her so much."

I can just imagine what a reunion that must have been.

## Coming to Grips with Reality

Dealing with reality can be like trying to play catch with a wrecking ball. One moment you seem to be getting a grip on your emotions and thought life, only to have them come crashing down the next. I remember sitting in my favorite chair one day, thinking about the incredible time B. A. and I had together. We had the kind of marriage so many people dream about but sadly don't.

All of a sudden reality knocked the wind out of my sails. *Betty Ann is gone and she's not coming back.* Even as I type this, I feel waves of sadness trying to creep in and take control of my thoughts. If these feelings are not checked by truth, there is only one outcome: to be held captive. Sometimes the toughest prison for us to escape from is the one in our own minds. No matter how devastating our life experiences may be, we can remain free, but it has to be intentional. We must take these thoughts captive and choose to set our minds on good things (2 Corinthians 10:5). We must take control of our thoughts, or our thoughts will control us.

If you are old enough to read this book, you are well aware of the fact that life can be very unfair. Deception is believing it has to be. We all know people who are morally bankrupt but seem to be blessed. On the other side of the coin, we know some godly people who have gone through some very difficult and unfair times. They pushed all the right buttons and pulled all the right levers and life still crashed in on them. The question many people ask is, if God is so good, why does He allow bad things to happen to good people?

Unfairness is not about the goodness of God. It is about the badness of humanity. It is the fruit produced by corrupted seed that was passed on to the human race through Adam, who chose to disobey God's warning not to eat from the tree of the knowledge of good and evil (Genesis 2:17). Because Adam willingly disobeyed God, his seed was corrupted and it infected the entire earthly realm where both good and bad people live.

Jesus said, "[The Father] makes His sun rise on the evil and on the good, and sends rain on the just and the unjust" (Matthew 5:45 NKJV). As long as we are in this tainted world's system, unfair things will happen to the nice and the nasty.

God is not concerned about getting us over something. He is focused on getting us through it. That is how a testimony is born. "Even *when I walk through* the darkest valley, I will not be afraid, for you are close beside me. Your rod and your staff protect and comfort me (Psalm 23:4 NLT, emphasis added). The Good Shepherd walks His sheep through dark valleys, not over them. Here is the good news: He always walks with us. We never walk alone. We can hang our hopes on that hook.

"My health may fail, and my spirit may grow weak, but God remains the strength of my heart, he is mine forever" (Psalm 73:26 NLT). Grief can leave us floundering at times, and it may appear like we may go under. The enemy of our souls will do everything within his power to try and make sure that happens. This is why I am so thankful for the "but God's we find in the scriptures. God never changes. He remains our strength no matter what life throws at us. The Lord keeps us on our feet by holding our hands during the times we find ourselves staggering, wondering if we are going to make it.

## Surviving Bad Reports

Life is filled with bad reports. Some are more severe than others, but they all can rattle us to the point where we think we may not make it. In order to survive our souls (minds, emotions, and wills) must be securely anchored. And Christ is the only anchor who will help us endure the ugliest of storms.

"This hope is a strong and trustworthy anchor for our souls. It leads us through the curtain into God's inner sanctuary" (Hebrews 6:19 NLT). We all have had moments when it felt like our grip on reality was slipping, leaving us feeling untethered from our spiritual moorings. That is why it is imperative that we get a firm hold on a very important biblical truth. Our survival is not about us holding on to God. Our survival comes from knowing that God is holding on to us.

"Don't be afraid, for I am with you. Don't be discouraged, for I am your God. I will strengthen you and help you. *I will hold you up with my victorious right hand*" (Isaiah 41:10 NLT, emphasis added).

The strength we need to get us through any and all troubles comes from God. He is our strength and secret hiding place. "God is our refuge and strength, always ready to help in times of trouble" (Palms 46:1 NLT). Pay close attention to what this verse does not say. It does not say God might help us *if* we find ourselves in trouble. It says that God is always ready to help us survive *when* we find ourselves in trouble.

We need to understand that just because we are Christians does not exempt us from getting bad reports. Bad reports can range from health issues, jobs, financial problems, divorce papers, children and grandchildren, and the list goes on. Being a devoted believer does not mean you will skate around on thick ice all the time. Sometimes we will find ourselves on thin ice. We can feel and hear the ice cracking underneath us. That is just the way it is in a broken and fallen world.

Getting through difficult times is a matter of focus. Having a free will, we can choose to focus on the bad reports or on God's promises. If we choose to set our attention on the bad reports, it will not be long until we lose sight of God's promises, especially the promise He made to never leave or forsakes us (Hebrews 13:5). When troubles hit, it is OK for us to look out, look down, or even look in, but we need to make sure our last look is up. We must intentionally set our focus on the author and finisher of our faith (Hebrews 12:2). He is our only salvation. No matter what life throws at us, it will never knock us out if we are looking up.

"The Lord is close to the brokenhearted; he rescues those whose spirits are crushed" (Psalm 34:18 NLT).

# 12

## *I Got to be Her Last in Everything*

WE WERE HAVING LUNCH AT A LOCAL WHATABURGER WHEN I gave Betty Ann her engagement ring. I know what many of you may be thinking, because I can read your mind like a cheap novel: *This guy is one romantic dude. Whataburger? Really?* Hey, if you have it, you have it, so why not flaunt it?

When she accepted the ring and placed it on her finger, tears slowly rolled down her cheeks. I held her hand and said, "B. A., I may not be your first in anything, but I want to be your last in everything." I had no idea how prophetic those words were going to be.

After having an unbelievable number of chemo treatments and radiations, and then fighting through COVID in the midst of it all, her body began to shut down. She fought courageously for six-and-a-half years and eight days. Not once during this entire time did she complain, question God, waver in her faith, or give up hope. She never got grumpy or difficult to be around. She was dying the same way she lived—in peace.

I have walked many people through the loss of a spouse over the last fifty years as a pastor. I have witnessed firsthand the emotional struggles one goes through when separated from his or her soulmate, covenant partner. The pain can be enfeebling. Things were different this time. I am the one wearing the sandals of grief. This is my road to walk, and no one can walk it for me, and only One can walk it with me. His name is Jesus.

## A Covenant of Oneness

I know what it is like to lose a sibling. My sister died from cervical cancer when she was just forty-one years old. My dad died from cancer and my mother from dementia complications. I also know the devastation of what losing a child can do to a parent's heart. I lost my firstborn daughter suddenly and unexpectedly when she was twenty-five years old. Melanie was only a few weeks away from having my first grandchild. They both entered God's presence together. And now I know what it feels like to lose a covenant partner. A part of you is separated from yourself, because you are one.

Oneness between a man and woman was God's idea. This uniqueness of covenant partners being one sets marriage apart from every relationship on this planet. Before there were fathers and mothers, this covenant-of-oneness was established. "Therefore a man shall leave his father and mother and be joined with his wife, and they shall become one flesh" (Genesis 2:24 NKJV).

The marriage covenant was established by God long before there were fathers and mothers or children. Our Creator was looking down the corridors of time and saw the difficulties and struggles that we would find ourselves in if we did not heed His word. We are not to become one with our children or our parents. This does not mean they are less than, it means our union with our marriage partner is more than. Our children are the ones who are to leave home to find and be joined with their soulmate. This in no way means that we don't love our children. We are not to become one with them. This has been God's plan from the beginning of time. Our marriage union will be dangerously compromised if we choose to disregard this truth about being one flesh with our spouse.

This covenant-of-oneness is what makes separation by death in this earthly realm so painful. What I said earlier needs to be repeated. Death of our spouse separates us from a part of ourselves. This is why we continue living, knowing that something is missing. And it is.

On a Wednesday morning at 4:58, I was going to experience this reality in a very real and personal way. My beautiful Proverbs Thirty-Two woman took her last breath in my presence, and her first breath in her Lord and Savior's presence.

### The Hard Decision That Had to Be Made

In a period of two months, I saw my sweet wife's earthly body deteriorate at warp speed. I had given my best to take care of her needs for six-and-a-half years, but now, her needs were more than I was able to provide. Where she was in her life's journey was obvious. I knew it, and I was certain she knew it as well. Palliative care was imminent, but I did not want to admit it. To me, placing someone in hospice sounds like the final straw. It signals the end.

The thoughts swirling through my head produced a kaleidoscope of emotions. *How do I bring up the subject? Will she think I'm giving up hope? Will talking about hospice care cause her to throw in the towel? Will she think I'm tired of taking care of her?* I cannot describe the battle that was raging inside me. It was horrific. The enemy was wreaking havoc with my thoughts and emotions.

For several weeks Betty Ann had told me that she did not feel well. What was going on inside her body was manifesting on her countenance. It was heart-wrenching to watch this happen and not be able to do a single thing to help. At this point in her battle with cancer, she was not able to do much of anything for herself. To watch her struggling was overpowering at times. Sometimes I had to walk out of the room before I lost it emotionally. I did not want her to see me cry.

The number-one thing that kept her fighting was her love for our girls, Brooke and Alex. The passionate love she had for our grandsons Carter, Cullen, and Mason kept her going when everything inside her was screaming to give up.

Betty Ann was about to win her battle over cancer. You see, death has no life for a child of God. The grave has lost its victory and death has lost its sting (1 Corinthians 15:54–56). Death is not the end for a believer; it is the beginning. We never die. We just change locations. We win!

I finally mustered enough courage to bring up the subject of hospice care. Her response was not what the enemy's lies had tried to convince me they would be. She did not receive it as being negative or me giving up on her. As a matter of fact, the opposite was true. It brought incredible relief to her. Even though she was not able to talk much, she was in total agreement with this decision. Her quick yes to pursuing hospice care destroyed all the negative thoughts and emotions I had about bringing up the subject. The enemy is a liar.

I immediately called a treasured friend, a man who happens to be my elder. He is also one of the best hospice chaplains in the state of Texas. Ken Branum was well aware of Betty Ann's physical struggles. He was vigilant in praying for her recovery and was always asking for an update on how she was doing. His sweet wife, Jody, was also a special friend to my B. A.

After we hung up, Ken went to work. Within hours there was a team from High Plains Hospice in our home. They were very knowledgeable and ever so kind. Their first priority was to make sure my beloved covenant partner was in no pain and was as comfortable as she possibly could be. I cannot believe how fast and precise things went from there. Before we knew it, all the equipment we needed for Betty Ann's care was in our home, hooked up and functioning. It was such a relief for me, and it was obvious it was for her as well.

All this happened on a Thursday. The following Wednesday, six days later, the love of my life went to be with her Lord and Savior, Jesus Christ. Death may have separated us in this earthly realm, but I did not lose her. You cannot lose someone when you know where she is.

Being separated from a part of yourself is incredibly painful. But the pain caused by this separation is part of the healing process. We must not cut short the mourning phases of healing. As Christians we do sorrow, but we do not sorrow as those who have no hope. We have hope!

"But I do not want you to be ignorant, brethren, concerning those who have fallen asleep, lest you sorrow as others who have no hope" (1 Thessalonians 4:13 NKJV). One of the biggest mistakes we can make is expecting others to grieve exactly the way we do. We are all wired differently. This is what makes us unique and special. We all grieve, but we all grieve differently.

# God Scripted the Ending Just for the Two of Us

The last forty-one minutes of our time together in this earthly realm had God's fingerprints all over it. I am absolutely convinced God scripted it just for us. It was the kind of physical separation you wish every husband and wife could experience when that time comes. Even though our last moments together were incredibly emotional, it was storybook in every way. Our final farewell epitomized our incredible covenant marriage.

I am convinced beyond any doubt that the numbers 4:17 (when Betty Ann's breathing pattern changed rapidly, and 4:58 (when she took her last breath in this earthly realm) have a greater significance than just a specific time that appears on a clock twice a day. To me they represent something far more consequential, as does the forty-one minutes between the two.

Let me see if I can explain what I am talking about. In biblical numerology, numbers found in the Bible convey a meaning outside the numerical value of the actual number being used. For instance, the number forty symbolizes a time of testing, trial, and then triumph. Here are a few examples. God flooded the earth with water because of man's sinfulness and rebellion against His word. How long did it rain? Forty days and forty nights. All the earth was destroyed by the flood with the exception of eight individuals: Noah, the builder of the Ark, and his family.

How long did Goliath taunt the Israelite army's resolve to fight? If your answer is forty days, give yourself a pat on the back.

God assigned Jonah to an evangelistic outreach to the people of Nineveh. Unless they repented, they would be destroyed in, you guessed it, forty days.

The number forty can also represent a generation of people. After being delivered from Egyptian bondage, the children of Israel wandered in the wilderness for forty years for their disobedience and rebellion against God. God did not allow them to possess the Promised Land. But He did reserve it for the next generation. I could write an entire book on the number forty. It is a significant number in the scriptures.

But forty is not the number of minutes between 4:17 am and 4:58 am, forty-one is. How significant is the number forty-one to the final moments before my beloved made her exit from this earthly realm into God's presence?

The number forty-one represents a beacon of hope for postponed dreams and promised lands. When you see the number forty in the scriptures, if you listen carefully, you will hear number forty-one in the background shouting, "I'm coming! Don't give up. I'm on my way!"

Here is a stunning observation: forty-one always follows forty. After reading that sentence, don't roll your eyes. Ask the Holy Spirit to help you connect the dots. Let me give you a hint. There is absolutely nothing God can't deliver us from. He can be trusted because He is trustworthy.

I mentioned earlier about Noah building the ark, and then the rain started falling. Water came down and water came up for forty days and forty nights, representing the judgment of God. Well, what comes after forty? Kudos to you if you said forty-one. On day forty-one the rains stopped. Never abandon ship when you are going through a difficult season. Your anchor (Jesus Christ) will always hold you steady in the midst of any storm (Hebrews 6:19). Keep reminding yourself that day forty-one is about to show up.

Moses self-exiled himself for forty years after he killed the Egyptian who was attacking one of his Jewish brothers. He spent forty years of his life in Pharaoh's house learning how to be somebody. He spent the next forty years on the backside of the wilderness learning how to be a nobody. It looks like Moses is destined to spend the rest of his life in self-exile. But wait. What number comes after forty? God gave Moses a second chance to do with His help what he tried to do on his own—deliver the Israelites from Egyptian bondage. Year forty-one came calling.

After leaving their life of slavery behind, the Israelites, led out of captivity by Moses, wandered in circles in the wilderness for forty years because of their stiff necks and rebellion against God's authority. But once again, year forty-one follows the number forty. Year forty-one came and a new generation entered the Promised Land.

Goliath bullied and taunted Israel's army for forty days, trying to get someone to step out of ranks to fight him. No one was willing to accept his challenge. It had all the earmarks of a surrender on the part of God's people. But day forty-one came. A young boy by the name of David stepped up and took out Goliath with a sling and a stone. The number forty-one represents the breaking of a new day.

I am convinced beyond any shadow of a doubt that God scripted the ending of Betty Ann's time here on earth just for the two of us. Even though being physically separated from the love of my life is incredibly hard, I can see God's hands all over it. The enemy of cancer thought it had won in the last forty minutes of my sweet Betty Ann's time in this physical realm. Not so! Minute forty-one was screaming out to both of us in the background, "I'm next! It's not over. It's just the beginning!"

On both ends of this forty-one-minute time frame are numbers that ooze with spiritual significance: 4:17 to 4:58. As I look back on this event, it seems like this time frame was actually a portal for me to see what was going on spiritually what I could not see with my physical eyes, especially looking back. God is in absolute control of all things. No matter how things may appear, or how hopeless the situation may seem, because God always wins, we win. As Betty Ann told me years ago, all we can do is win, or learn. We never lose.

**Divine Time: 4:17 to 4:58 am**

Let's begin with the number four. Four is the number for created order. This is why we have four directions, north, south, east, and west. We also have four seasons, winter, spring, summer, and fall.

What does the number one represent? One is the number for God. It is only divisible by itself. It is independent of any other numeral yet composes them all. God is alone in His sovereignty, but He expresses Himself as the Father, Son, and Holy Spirit.

The number seven represents completeness, fullness, and perfection. Seven days is a complete week. God created the heavens and the earth in six days. He rested on the seventh day when everything was in its assigned place (Genesis 2:1–2). God's rest day was Adam's first day. Adam began his relationship with God in rest.

Five is directly linked to God's grace and mercy. It is a number that symbolizes God's kindness and favor to humankind. And the number eight means fullness and the beginning of a new order or creation.

I have only skipped the rock over the surface of the water in defining these numbers 4:17 to 4:58. Biblical numerology is fascinating. Can you imagine the insights into the spiritual realm we have forfeited simply because we have not paid attention to numbers' "outside" meanings? And there is a real possibility that we have never been taught or have confused biblical numerology with the divination of astrology. What I have shared should give you a little insight into how numbers convey a meaning outside their numerical value.

When I look at what these numbers represent by themselves, and then together, it paints a beautiful picture of how God scripted the ending just for me and my beloved soulmate. On April 13, 2022, Betty Ann's number of days on this earth were completed. The enemy of cancer was gloating because it thought it had won, but in the background, you could hear grace screaming, "I'm here! It's not over. Your life is just beginning."

To make this moment even more special, a dove (a symbol of peace) outside our window started cooing. It was 4:58 in the morning, the very moment when the love of my life took her final flight. Here is what makes this moment so special. My sweet B. A., my trusted covenant partner, soulmate, friend, companion in mischief, finished her race here on earth at a sunrise, not a sunset.

## Time of Departure Was at Hand

I knew the time for my beloved's departure was only minutes away. It was just the three of us: me, B. A., and the Lord. I know what death looks like. I have seen it more times than I care to remember. Through tears and cyclonic emotions, I began to sing over my sweet soulmate. I thanked her for being a faithful, trusted covenant partner, an incredible wife, a phenomenal mother to the girls, and a special Nanny Ann to our grandsons. I kept my left hand placed lightly on her chest because I knew she was about to draw her last breath on this side of eternity. I wanted her last earthly touch to be mine.

Her left eye remained closed but her right eye was staring straight ahead, slightly upward. All of a sudden, her gaze was locked on me. I never saw her eye shift in my direction. Her last look at me spoke volumes. During our years together, I have caught her staring at me many times. I would usually say something like, "What are you looking at, Missy?"

She would say, "At the man of my dreams. I'm so glad you're in my life. You will always be my cowboy."

This time she did not say anything audibly, or make a facial expression, or twitch her fingers. She just lay there motionless with a peaceful stare. But I knew what she was saying. I could hear her soul speaking loudly. At 4:58 am, my sweet wife took her last breath in this physical realm and then took her first breath in eternity.

She was absent from her body, but present with her Lord (2 Corinthians 5:8). My prayer request was answered. My wish had come true. God had given me the desires of my heart. The words I spoke to her in Whataburger that day when I gave her a ring had come true. Our heavenly Father allowed me to be the last thing, in everything, in her life: The last look, the last touch, the last word, and the last kiss. I can't thank my heavenly Father enough for giving me that special moment that will be forever treasured in my heart.

B. A., you will always be my Proverbs Thirty-Two woman. I will never break my covenant with you. I will love you all the days of my life. And I will continue to wear my wedding band and covenant ring in honor of you. You're still my covenant partner.

I can't wait to see your smiling face again and hear you say, "Hello, Cowboy; let me show you around."

I will see you soon, sweetie. Save me a seat (J21).

# EPILOGUE

I spent a lot of time mulling over how to bring this book to an end. Then the truth hit me like a ton of bricks; there is no way I can. I am left with a warehouse full of memories, and every one of them triggers another chapter. To be frankly honest, Betty Ann was the one who wrote this book. It was written by her life. And what she left behind will live on in my heart and in the hearts of those who knew her until that great reunion we all will have in glory someday. That special day may be sooner than we expect.

I began *My Proverbs -Thirty-Two Woman* with this scripture: "Who can find a virtuous and capable wife? She is more precious than rubies. Her husband can trust her, and she will greatly enrich his life. She brings him good, not harm, all the days of her life" (Proverbs 31:10–12 NLT). This one verse sums up the life Betty Ann and I had together. I found a treasure. She was easy to trust; she greatly enriched my life; she brought me good and not harm; and she loved me for the rest of her life. She was a lady of noble character.

I realize there may be those who read this book and think I may have fudged a little with my praise for Betty Ann. The truth is, I have used a lot of restraint in describing her as my Proverbs -Thirty-Two woman. That lady was indescribable. She was the most honest and legit person I have ever met. No one on this earth ever loved me like this lady loved me. And she wanted me to know it, not just by words but by her actions. She always made sure I knew I was number one on her list of priorities. This was true before we got married, and even more so after we married. She made it easy to love her in return.

When Betty Ann said, "I do," she meant it. There was not an ounce of pretense in this lady. The marriage covenant we entered into was for both of our lives. She made a commitment to love me for the rest of her life, and I made a vow to love her for the rest of my life. And she did just that. I will do the same.

One of the most important constructs of a great marriage is trust. If trust is ever dented or broken, it is difficult to have it restored. As author Frank K. Sonnenberg (*Listen to Your Conscience: That's Why You Have One*) said, "Trust is like blood pressure. It's silent, vital to good health, and if abused, it can be deadly."

Trust leads to more trust. This incredible woman made it easy for me to trust her. Never once did I have any doubts about her love and commitment to me. Never! That is so liberating.

The way she lived her life and the way she loved me ignited an insatiable desire deep within me to be the best person I can possibly be. I want to be the kind of man she believed and said I was. It is amazing how much influence a good wife has on her husband. If I had to sum up the impact my Proverbs Thirty-Two woman had on me, I would say it this way. I may not be the man I should be, or even want to be, but praise God, I am not the man I used to be. Her love and unwavering commitment to me is what made the difference in my life. She made it so easy for me to love her.

The peace and solace I have is in knowing my sweet bride is no longer in pain. I watched her fight vigorously for six-and-a-half years that insidious enemy called cancer. She never gave up hope because she knew she could not lose. If physical healing manifested while she was in this earthly realm, wonderful. If it meant she would be escorted to heaven to receive her forever healing, so be it. Either way, she wins. This truth is what sustains me, and keeps me on my feet as I walk this path of emotional healing. As I said earlier, it is a road no one can walk for me. And only One can walk it with me.

The song "Scars in Heaven" by Casting Crowns has really ministered to me during this season of physical separation from my covenant partner. I encourage you to give it a listen if you have not heard it. Here are just a few words of this song.

> 'Cause there's a wound here in my heart
> where something's missing,
> And they tell me it's gonna heal in time.
> But I know you're in a place where all your
> Wounds have been erased,
> And knowing yours are healed are healing mine.

Knowing my forever Proverbs -Thirty-Two woman is healed and in the forever presence of her Lord and Savior, Jesus Christ is what God is using to heal me.

In my thoughts I am always talking to B. A. My emotions are always feeling her sweet presence. Do I grieve? Absolutely, but not as those who have no hope (1 Thessalonians 4:13). In my soul, I know she is healed and at peace. And knowing she is healed is healing me. You're never ready to say goodbye, so I'll just say, See you again soon, sweetheart.

Always your Cowboy,
J.21

Grief, I have learned, is really just love. It's all the love you want to give, but cannot. All that unspent love gathers up in the corners of your eyes, the lump in your throat, and that hollow part of your chest. Grief is just love with no place to go. (Canadian author Jamie Anderson)

# APPENDIX

*Insights into Grieving*

Grief is not an option in this earthly realm. There is no way for us to opt out of going through tough times. No one is immune from seasons of mourning. It is a reality that everyone will have to deal with sometime or another in their lives. Even though we all grieve, our experiences will be unique to us because we are all wired differently emotionally. There is no specific time frame or particular sequence for grief to run its course. I want to repeat what I said earlier in this book. You may never get over the pain from your loss, and that is perfectly OK. But never forget God's promise to you; no matter how challenging your grief season may be, He will get you through it.

Wherever you are in the process of being restored and emotionally healthy again, God will always be with you—always. He will never run out on you or walk away. He has never thrown up His hands and quit on anybody. Don't worry about having enough strength to hold on to God's hand. Separation caused by death can weaken our emotional stability to the point where we don't think we can hold on to anything. Relax in the hand that is holding you—His. Your emotional weakness will never abate His power and strength.

There is no part of us that is not touched by the tentacles of grief. Our entire souls (how we think and feel and what we do) will be engaged in our mourning experiences. It will affect us spiritually, emotionally, and physically. Don't think something is wrong with you if you do not grieve like other people. You are not them, and they are not you. Your path of grief can only be walked by you. But you will never walk it alone. Jesus will always be with you.

The covenant of oneness creates and sustains a spiritual connection between husbands and wives. This spiritual truth was established in the very beginning of time by our Creator. "This explains why a man leaves his father and mother and is joined to his wife, and *the two are united into one*" (Genesis 2:24 NLT, emphasis added). This is the reason we never get over losing our spiritual mates: Death separates us from a part of ourselves. Even though we may never get over our loss, God has given His word that He will get us through our pain.

## *The One Holding Your Hand through Your Grieving Season Is the God of All Comfort*

Knowing the God of all comfort is holding my hand is what keeps my sanity from taking a hiatus. "Blessed be the God and Father of our Lord Jesus Christ, the Father of mercies and *God of all comfort*, who *comforts us in all our tribulation*, that we may be able to comfort those who are in any trouble, with the comfort with which we ourselves are comforted by God" (2 Corinthians 1:3–4 NKJV, emphasis added). There is no level of grief a person will ever experience that will be outside the parameters of God's ability to provide them with comfort. He is the God of all comfort.

Being a pastor for more than fifty years has afforded me many opportunities to minister comfort to those who are hurting from the death of a loved one. I have seen people who were sky-high one moment, thinking their grieving season was over, only to find themselves at the bottom of the barrel the next. This is the emotional rollercoaster one can find themselves on when death brings a physical separation from loved ones. You may find yourself going through sudden or extreme changes in a brief period of time. There are no off ramps, either.

There is one difference this time. I am the one going through what I have helped others navigate their way through for the last half century. What a ride it is, too. Even though I do feel there has been some healing in my soul, I know my grieving season is not over. My ticket has been punched and I have to ride it out. There are no shortcuts. I am obliged to follow the same counsel I have given to others who have worked their way through grief.

I think it would only be right (maybe even helpful) if I shared a little more inside information with you. As I write *My Proverbs Thirty-Two Woman*, it has only been ten months since my wife went to be with the Lord. There are moments when I have a total meltdown as I type this manuscript. There are times when I have to walk away from my computer, because the grief I am feeling is so overwhelming. Some of the stories I have written about have triggered some fond memories that will be indelibly imprinted in my innermost being—forever.

There is one reason I want you to know this. What you are reading is not coming from years of being healed. I am walking this path of grief as you read this book. My mind, emotions, and will are raw and very sensitive. These insights into the grieving process I am sharing with you are something I'm going through myself *right now*. They are coming from a deep understanding of how difficult the grieving process can be, because they come out of the crucible of my own experience from being physically separated from the love of my life, my covenant partner. Keep reading; we will cry together.

Here are three insights that may help bring comfort to your soul as you fight to maintain your emotional equilibrium caused by the death of a loved one.

## 1. Grief Is the Byproduct of Love

The only way not to grieve is never love. How unnatural that would be. The chances are great that the deeper you love someone, the greater the pain you will experience when death separates you physically. Grief is actually a good thing. I know that may sound weird, or even heartless to those who are mourning a loss. But it is the truth. Grief takes us through a series of emotions that is beneficial for our healing. The grieving cycle can be repeated over and over again. There is no time limit. Emotions do not come in a specific order, either. Sometimes they will sucker punch you when you least expect it. A memory, a smell, a sound, a picture can trigger an emotional episode, oftentimes ambushing you without warning.

Never think God will disown you if, during your grieving process, you express doubt, anger, fear, mood swings, or a kaleidoscope of other emotions. Your feelings will constantly change. This is why grieving can be so challenging. You're up one moment, down the next—up and down, just like a yoyo on a string. No matter how severe these moments may be, keep reminding yourself, God still has a hold of my hand, and He will never let go.

When you find yourself in the throes of an emotional meltdown, the enemy will try to convince you that you have no faith. If you did, you would not be in the emotional mess you find yourself. Satan will do everything in his power to make you believe the sun will never shine again. I have said this several times already, and you will probably read it again before you finish this section on insights into grief. When (not if) this happens, intentionally place your focus on the one whose hand is holding you. This is a truth you need to remind yourself of as many times as needed.

Shedding tears does not show a lack of faith. It is utilizing the built-in equipment our Creator blessed us with at birth—tear ducts—a built-in drainage system. Without them we might drown. Both men and women have been gifted with nasolacrimal ducts. It is OK to cry. Voltaire said, "Tears are the silent language of grief."

"And *God will wipe away every tear from their eyes*; there *shall be no more* death nor sorrow, *nor crying*. There shall be no more pain, for the former things have passed away" (Revelation 21:4 NKJV, emphasis added).

Never forget that your heavenly Father is your safe place. He has given all His children permission to crawl up in His lap any time they need a safe place, a place they can go and cry without receiving counsel, being lectured, or preached to, a place where they can go and be lovingly held. "*God's a safe-house* for the battered, *a sanctuary* during bad times. The moment you arrive, you relax; you're never sorry you knocked" (Psalm 9:9 MSG, emphasis added).

I was watching an old TV western series called *Cheyanne*. During this particular episode, a lady's husband had been shot and killed. After the perpetrator had been captured and dealt with, the sheriff met with the woman in his office. He brought her up-to-date on how justice had been metered out. She was emotional during this short briefing.

When all was said and done, the sheriff said to her, "You need to go home now, miss, and get over it." This was not my first time to watch this scene, but it was the first time I had heard these word: "Go home and get over it."

Even though it was a TV program, I remember how repulsed I was by the sheriff's words to this grieving widow. You lose a love one, and the counsel you are given, is to get over it. I realize this was just a scene in this specific episode of *Cheyanne*, but nonetheless, it is the counsel so many people who are grieving get from those who do not understand that grief is a byproduct of love. Just get over it? Maybe not in this lifetime. But one thing is for sure, God will get us through it. He is the only One who can.

## 2. *Grieving Is the Way Emotional Pain Is Vented*

Unless there is a way for us to vent our hurts and pains caused by the physical separation of a loved one, we run the risk of imploding. Stuffed hurts can do irreparable harm. To heal from emotional wounds, a person must have the freedom and permission to express their inner hurts. If not, we take the chance of perpetuating their emotional pain: Hurt people hurt people. People who find themselves in a grieving season need to be given time and space to express their mental anguish.

Grieving is the normal response to a major loss. It keeps us from disintegrating emotionally. Suppressed feelings can lead to greater and more dangerous issues that may even cause physical harm. "Beloved, I pray that you may prosper in all things and be in health, just as your soul prospers" (3 John 1:2 NKJV). This verse reveals that there is a close connection with our souls and bodies. Our soul is our minds, emotions, and wills: The way we think, how we feel, and what we do. If we are not thriving in our souls, it could lead to physical repercussions.

Varying degrees of depression is a common denominator that all grieving people share. But it will be expressed differently, because our Creator wired in our uniqueness at conception. We do a person great harm when we demand that he or she must grieve the way we do, since there is no set order in the grieving process. Our emotions are in a state of flux, constantly changing. One moment it may seem like someone turned the light on (it's a new day), and then, all of a sudden, the light is switched off. We are left to grope in the darkness of our thoughts and emotions.

Since it is impossible to control the process of mourning, there is no way for us to be thoroughly prepared for every stage that we may find ourselves going through. We are constantly coming to forks in the road, and sometimes it feels like we have no choice which path we take. This is why it is strongly suggested that we do not make major decisions too early in our grieving process. Our thoughts and emotions change like the hands on a clock. Because our feelings are fickle, it is wise to wait until we have more emotional stability before we make any resolutions. There can be severe consequences to the choices we make. This is wise counsel for those who have the tendency to fly by the seat-of-the-pants.

Mourning is an outward expression of inner grief. Let me say it this way. Grief is our feelings; mourning is expressing these feelings. Crying is not a sign of weakness or a lack of faith. The shedding of tears is the way we vent our inner hurts and pains. It is perfectly OK to cry. It is also OK not to cry. At this point in my personal grieving process, I find myself crying several times a day. Tears start flowing when I find a love note that I wrote to my precious wife that she kept in her treasure trove of keepsakes. There are times I look at a picture and begin to cloud up. A thought or memory may flash across my mind that causes an outward expression of the inner pain I am feeling. There is a plethora of other trigger events that can cause the tears to flow.

I have a friend who is going through the same grieving process that I am. One day he asked me if I ever cried. I told him I shed tears every day.

I will never forget what he said: "I have not cried one tear yet."

Does that mean that I am grieving the right way and he is not? Does that mean I should be grieving the way he is? Neither of us are wrong by the way we are venting the pain of our losses. We are separate individuals. Because we are emotionally wired differently by our Creator, we will mourn according to our bents. We must allow a person to be who he or she is.

Our bodies need a way to let our negative emotions out and not suppress them. There are many ways we can do this. But the best way is to take them to the Lord. In no way am I discounting the incredible benefits that come from wise counsel. We need to be connected to trusted people who have patience and are willing to listen to us as we express our hurts and pains. But our first go-to should be our God. The more go-betweens we eliminate the better. Our heavenly Father has all the answers, and He is the only one who can impart peace to the emotional war that rages inside us. He is a wonderful listener. Sometimes we do not need answers, we just need for someone to listen to us vent our feelings. "Be still, and know that I am God" (Psalm 46:10 NKJV).

### 3. Grief Is What God Uses to Heal Us, Spirit, Soul, and Body

There is no right or wrong way to deal with loss. But there is one guaranteed way we can be victorious over our pain and heartache. And that is by leaning on our relationship with God. He is not only our hope, He is our only hope. "The Lord is *close to the brokenhearted; he rescues* those whose spirits are crushed" (Psalm 34:18 NLT, emphasis added). These are comforting words. God will never cast us aside as being hopeless.

Jesus wept and grieved when his friend Lazarus died. "Therefore, *when Jesus saw her weeping,* and the Jews who came with her *weeping,* He groaned in the spirit and was troubled. And He said, 'Where have you laid him?' They said to Him, 'Lord, come and see.' *Jesus wept*" (John 11:33–35 NKJV, emphasis added). Jesus was moved by Mary's tears. He felt the pain she was experiencing over the loss of her brother. Her grief and sorrow moved Him to tears. Jesus wept. God sees our brokenness. He feels our crushed spirits, and it touches His heart.

There may be times when the pain over the loss of your loved one is so debilitating you think you will never laugh again. When things seem hopeless, God shows up with a timely word that provides strength for our sagging spirits: "God blesses you who are hungry now, for you will be satisfied. God blesses *you who weep now,* for *in due time you will laugh*" (Luke 6:21 NLT; emphasis added). Eventually at an appropriate time, laughter will greet you again. Inner healing is on the way, so do not give up. When you feel like you're at the end of your rope, tie a prayer knot and hold on.

In the book of Isaiah, there is a verse that I have shared with people over the last fifty years who found themselves in the valley of the shadow of death. Today it is not a simple quote in an attempt to lift a person's spirit. It is to remind myself that an exchange is coming.

The first part of this verse reads like this: "To all who mourn in Israel, he will give a crown of beauty for ashes, a joyous blessing instead of mourning, festive praise instead of despair" (Isaiah 61:3 NLT). This is God's promise to those of us who are in the process of healing from our losses. There is coming an exchange of ashes for a crown of beauty, joy for mourning, and praise for despair. Do not allow a languid spirit to take control of the emotional steering wheel of your life.

Before Jesus went to the cross, He told his disciples that He was going away. He would be returning to His father. This news upset them. I'm sure they were stunned by this announcement. These men believed they would be with Him in this earthly realm forever. Now He's going away. What would they do when He leaves? Does this mean they have to go back to square one? Who will lead them? To lift their spirits, Jesus told them that when He departed, his Father would send the Holy Spirit to be in them and with them forever.

Jesus consoled His disciples with these words: "I am leaving you with *a gift—peace of mind and heart.* And the peace I give is a gift the world cannot give. So don't be troubled or afraid" (John 14:27 NLT, emphasis added). The promise Jesus made to His disciples was not just for them. It is for us today as well. Knowing He will never leave us will give us traction when our emotions are slipping and sliding in all directions. We are not and never will be alone! The world cannot give us everything we need during our times of grieving, but God can.

I received a card of encouragement recently from two of my dear friends, Fred and Irene Hughes. These two saints live in another town, but I have the opportunity to see them on a regular basis. It was a sweet card with the intent to lift my spirts. And it certainly did. What captured my attention were the words written on front of the card: "Life is fragile—handle with prayer." I'll bet you can guess what I did. Yes, I cried! God is using this grieving season to bring healing to me: spirit, soul, and body. He has promised to do the same for you.

## Life Is Fragile–Handle with Prayer

If you do not have a personal relationship with Jesus Christ that you can lean on, or you are not sure, this would be a good time to take care of that. The only thing that keeps this from happening, is you.

The following is a model prayer that can be prayed by anyone seeking salvation and emotional healing.

## Prayer for Salvation

Lord Jesus, I need the assurance that it is well with my soul. Life is brief and I will spend eternity somewhere: With You or separated from You, forever. You said: "If you [I] confess with your [my] mouth the Lord Jesus and believe in your [my] heart that God has raised Him from the dead, you [I] will be saved. For with the heart one believes unto righteousness, and with the mouth confession is made unto salvation. For whoever calls on the name of the Lord shall be saved" (Romans 10:9–10, 13 NKJV, emphasis added).

I am doing what You said I needed to do in order to be in right standing with You. And I believe I can trust what You say. I confess my sins and accept and receive Jesus Christ as my Lord and Savior. By faith I exchange my old sinful life for a new creation life only You can give. I have done what You told me to do. I have confidence that You will do what You said You would do. Thank You for hearing my prayer, forgiving me of my sins, and making me part of Your forever family. I belong to You now. In Jesus's name, amen.

## Prayer for Healing

Father, I need Your healing touch. My soul is in turmoil at this moment. My thoughts and my feelings are holding me hostage. There are times I feel like I will never be free from the pain I am experiencing because of the loss of my loved one, _____ . Because I belong to You, I have permission to exchange my fear for Your peace; my sorrow for Your joy; my brokenness for Your healing; my loneliness for Your presence; my confusion for Your assurance; my inferiorities for Your confidence; my ashes for Your beauty; my despair for Your praise; my lack for Your completeness; my rejection for Your acceptance; my doubt for Your confidence; my _____ for Your _____; my _____ for Your _____.

Your promise to me is that I will never have to walk this path alone. You gave me Your word that You would never leave or forsake me (Hebrews 13:5). You will never turn Your heart from me. Guard my heart and mind, Father. Keep my mind fixed on my Lord and Savior, Jesus Christ.

"So *it is impossible for God to lie* for we know that *his promise* and *his vow* will never change! *And now we have run into his heart to hide ourselves in his faithfulness*" (Hebrews 6:18 The Passion Translation, emphasis added).

# MY FIRST ANNIVERSARY NOTE

## *To My Beloved Betty Ann*

I had no idea how blessed I was when God brought you into my life. He knew exactly what I needed when He created you. As you were being formed in your mother's womb, I can hear a voice in my head saying, "Now this one will fit Wayne just right." You are the perfect piece that makes me complete. I remember the day I saw you as someone I wanted in my life, to be more than my friend—I saw you as my soulmate, my marriage covenant partner.

For me, you define 1 John 4:18 "There is no fear in love, but perfect love casts out fear" (NKJV). There is no fear in our relationship. I have the freedom to share with you my dreams, my successes, and even my failures without fear.

Your honor and respect for me nurtures my desire to love you sacrificially. I am committed to helping you succeed in whatever you feel your calling is and to do whatever I can to help you realize your dreams.

You will never have to question my faithfulness to you or my commitment to take care of you and Alex. When it is all said and done, I want you to be able to say, *"Father, thank you for Wayne; he was not only my best friend, he was a faithful husband and wonderful father. I am a better person because of him."*

This was written and given to my beloved Betty Ann in October 2002. We were celebrating our first year together as covenant partners. This means much more to me now than it did then. I will always honor this commitment.

# A PROMISE FULFILLED

I was cleaning out a closet and found this note that I had written to B. A. on Mother's Day, dated May 10, 2020. I do not think I discovered it by accident.

Happy Mother's Day to my Proverbs 32
lady, one-of-a-kind woman.
It was a good day for this ole boy when you finally said yes!
I know that I'm not what I should be at times, or ought to be,
But praise the Lord, I'm not what I used
to be, and it's because of you.
You have made me a better man.
I sure pray these last nineteen-plus years have been as good
For you as they've been for me. I know I fall short sometimes,
But I do try to demonstrate to you by my actions
How much I love and respect you.
You are a strong woman of faith and unbelievable courage.
Very seldom does a day go by when I don't
Brag on you to someone.
I've told you many times, you are my hero!
I pray your day today will be awesome, peaceful, and relaxing.

I'm thankful Brooke and Carter got to be
Here to honor you today for being their mother,
And grandmother. I know Alex is here
In spirit.
The book is coming, sister!
Happy Mother's Day.

You Still Make My Heart Smile—J.21

Promise fulfilled.

# ABOUT THE AUTHOR

Wayne Kniffen is a gifted communicator who uses humor in his presentations, especially the harder and more difficult the subject may be. He is convinced that people will swallow more truth if they can laugh it down. His humor and quick wit make him a crowd favorite. He loves the challenge of taking that which is simply profound and making it profoundly simple.

In writing this book, Kniffen is fulfilling a promise he made to his precious wife years ago: "Someday I am going to write a book about you, because I want people to know just how special you are. God gave me an incredible gift when he blessed me with you. Thank you for being my Proverbs Thirty-Two woman."

Kniffen has been a senior pastor for more than fifty years. In this last season of his life, he has become a prolific writer, penning more than twelve books. Even though he is now in his senior years, he believes it is the most productive season of his life. The desire of his heart is to let what he leaves live on. He is convinced that this is the only thing that really matters in this earthly realm: Leaving something that gives life and imparts hope to those who come behind us.

*My Proverbs Thirty-Two Woman* was written only weeks after Kniffen's beloved covenant partner, Betty Ann, went to be with Jesus. You can feel his emotions on every page.

Contact Information
waynekniffen@outlook.com
Visit his website: wkniffen.com.

Printed in the United States
by Baker & Taylor Publisher Services